Recipes from a Rectory Kitchen

Recipes from a Rectory Kitchen

Joyce Critchlow

Illustrated by Molly Dowell

MarshallPickering
An Imprint of HarperCollins*Publishers*

Marshall Pickering is an Imprint of
HarperCollins*Religious*
Part of HarperCollins*Publishers*
77–85 Fulham Palace Road, London W6 8JB

First published in Great Britain
in 1994 by Marshall Pickering

1   3   5   7   9   10   8   6   4   2

A catalogue record for this book is
available from the British Library

ISBN 0 551 02804-1

Phototypeset by Harper Phototypesetters Limited,
Northampton, England
Printed and bound in Great Britain by
The Bath Press, Bath, Avon

To the Memory
of my Father,
who prepared the soil
and gave me an abiding love of plants,
and of my Mother,
who taught me the sheer joy of hospitality
and unravelled many mysteries of cooking.

W.H.C.   M.E.C.

Requiescant in Pace

Contents

Introduction

The earth is the Lord's, and the fulness thereof; the world, and they that dwell therein. (Psalm 24:1)

This little book is about that fulness – natural, good, wholesome food: simple food, naturally grown and prepared into nourishing meals.

Except where otherwise stated, each recipe caters for four people.

As far as possible, I've used fresh ingredients in season for each month's recipes. But nowadays the twin advantages of freezers and large supermarkets make it possible to brighten even the darkest, shortest winter days with a variety of summer produce. At the breezy, high altitude of Derbyshire's Peak District, where in normal winters snow often blankets the garden to a depth of several feet, my standing vegetables can be locked in semi-permafrost for weeks on end. So you'll see from several recipes that my freezer more than earns its keep.

For, in our short summers, I grow a variety of fruit and vegetables, in addition to more than three hundred herbs. I have the extra pleasure of sowing much of my food, the virtue of exercise in tending it – and, alongside the sheer delight of cooking, eating and sharing it, the comfort of knowing the plants haven't been subjected to artificial chemicals; because, like Caesar, I've always been told to be wary of the 'Ides' – pesticides, herbicides, insecticides, and the rest.

1

I hope the sheer fun *I have in growing, preparing and eating these recipes will embrace you, too. Enjoy every flavour to the full – and, in coming through these twelve months with me, I invite you also to glimpse something of this parsonage-house and my memories and travels, which have played a large part in producing these dishes.*

Joyce Critchlow
King Sterndale
April 1993

CONVERSION TABLES

Dry

IMPERIAL	METRIC
1 oz	25 g
2 oz	50 g
3 oz	75 g
4 oz	100–125 g
5 oz·	150 g
6 oz	175 g
7 oz	200 g
8 oz	225 g
9 oz	250 g
10 oz	275 g
11 oz	300 g
12 oz	350 g
13 oz	375 g
14 oz	400 g
15 oz	425 g
16 oz	450 g

Wet

CAPACITY	
1 fl. oz	25 ml
2 fl. oz	50 ml
5 fl. oz	150 ml
10 fl. oz	300 ml
15 fl. oz	400 ml
20 fl. oz	600 ml
35 fl. oz	1 litre

January

The Old Vicarage —
King Sterndale
January

---

*And God said: 'While the earth remaineth,
seedtime and harvest, and cold and heat, and
summer and winter, and day and night,
shall not cease.'
(Genesis 8:22)*

January

STARTERS

Super-Soup • Blackberries in Cheese • Winter Salad

SAVOURY LIGHT LUNCHEON /
SUPPER DISHES

---

*Cheese Toasties • Chicken Stir-Fry
• Ham and Eggs •*

DINNER (MAIN COURSE DISHES)

---

*Sausage Supreme • Meat and Vegetable Pie
• Fish and Rice •*

DESSERTS

---

*Auntie Betty's Flapjacks • Chewy Shortcake
• Demonsdale Custard •*

BREAD AND CAKES

Wholemeal Bread • Sterndale Sponge • Brioches

HERBS OF THE MONTH

Bay • Sweet Violet • Lemon Verbena • Caraway

Except where otherwise stated, each recipe caters for four people

---

I suppose it's a bit unusual to have a battle with pheasants, but each January sees the local lordly cock with his innocent-looking harem of demure browny hens trying to race me to the Jerusalem artichokes. They know full well that the December frosts have mellowed these delicious tubers. We settle for a 75–25 split, in favour of the grower.

For us, this is usually the month of snow, snow which in a hard winter blocks the drive for weeks on end and makes the freezer and double-pantry extra-welcome. I dig a tunnel through the largest drifts, and wait for the thaw. Some friends come over to tell me they took the train to Manchester the other day, just to recall what green grass looks like.

A gale blows up, ahead of the milder weather. Power-lines, heavy with accumulated ice, collapse; and everyone except me thinks it's so romantic to eat by candlelight. Fortunately one can cook a lot on an open fire . . .

STARTERS

A quick soup, which I concocted for a surprise dinner party in 1987, is

Super-Soup

½ pint chicken and garlic stock

Basic stock recipe
1 chicken, 2½ –3 lb
the bird's cleaned giblets
1½ oz butter
1 clove garlic, chopped
1 celery stick
½ lb parsnips
salt and pinch of parsley to taste

Place all ingredients in a pan and cover with cold water. Bring slowly to boil. Cover with tight-fitting lid and simmer for 2–3 hours. Skim off fat, and strain liquid.
To the liquid add:
½ lb leeks, cleaned and sliced into rounds
½ lb Jerusalem artichokes, cleaned and chopped.

Return to the pan, and bring to boil. Simmer for 30–35 minutes. Serve piping hot with croutons – or with wholemeal bread toasted on the fire around a soup-pan which gets blacker by the minute!

I try to have blackberries in the freezer for most of the year. But any soft fruits in the freezer can be used. A delicious starter for warmer days, and one of my favourites, is

Blackberries in Cheese

½ lb blackberries, drained
1 lb soft curd cheese
pinch of lemon verbena
sugared violets to decorate

Blend the fruit into the cheese, flavour with the lemon verbena, and serve in glass sundae dishes, topped with sugared violets. Enjoy the juice as a hot bedtime drink.

There's great satisfaction in filling a colander with fresh greens, in the middle of winter. Even on snowy days, after a forage along the windowsills and in the greenhouse, I can find enough greenery for the basis of a

Winter Salad

Leaves of scented geranium
rue
horehound
landcress
parsley
rosemary
myrtle
feverfew (2–3
leaves only)
winter lettuce
chicory
chickweed
marjoram
evergreen mint
French sorrel
dandelion
hyssop

These fresh greens, tossed in olive oil, augmented with one small tin (7 oz) of tuna flakes, and topped with swirls of natural yoghurt, also make a delicious and quick luncheon or supper. And light luncheons are the order of the day in these months of long nights. Scant winter sunshine does not encourage one to use extra calories in cooking elaborate midday dishes.

LIGHT SAVOURY DISHES

Derbyshire is rich in cheese, perhaps that's why we eat so much. There's Blue Stilton, Sage Derby and a 'plain' Derby cheese in which the curd is stained yellow with marigold petals. I use this last cheese for

Cheese Toasties

½ lb Derby cheese
butter
white pepper
2 tsp landcress or watercress, chopped
2 tbsp thick cream
4 slices of wholemeal bread, toasted

Dice the cheese and put into a double saucepan which has been well-greased with butter. Season with pepper and cress. Add the cream. Melt slowly over low heat, stirring as the cheese softens. Increase the heat gently until the mixture bubbles. Spread on slices of wholemeal toast and brown under the grill.

I wouldn't be without my trusty stock-pot, but there are so many more dishes it supplies than casseroles, delicious though they are. One of our favourite quickies is

Chicken Stir-Fry

10 oz brown rice
2 tbsp olive oil
2 lb chicken, cooked in the stock-pot, then diced
2 garlic cloves, chopped not crushed
2 oz parsnips, diced
4 oz chicory, sliced
2 oz sultanas
2 oz nuts (walnuts for preference) chopped
salt and pepper to taste
parsley to garnish

Cook rice for 30 minutes; keep hot. Heat the oil in a strong pan (or wok). Stir-fry chicken, garlic, parsnips and chicory for 5–7 minutes. Add sultanas, nuts and seasoning and fry for a further two minutes. Stir in rice, heat thoroughly, and serve immediately with a parsley garnish.

For days when friends pop in unexpectedly, or I haven't time for cooking rice, I dish up a favourite of my father's. We've never got around to calling it anything but

Ham and Eggs

For each person:
1 round of wholemeal toast
1 egg
oil for frying
1 thick slice of boiled ham
generous pinch of caraway seed

While the bread is toasting, fry the eggs to your taste in a very little oil. Place the ham on the toast and top with egg. Garnish with caraway.

So simple, it's hardly a recipe! I never cook this dish without happy memories of those post-war days when we kept a couple of pigs each year. Nowadays our ham is bought, but from an impeccably-organic farmer whose pigs range free.

MAIN COURSE DISHES

I seemed to be at university for half a lifetime, being involved with several colleges, in each of which were dedicated professors – dedicated, that is, to broadening my theological outlook, or so budding theologians were informed. And who was I to argue? I enjoyed it immensely.

University life, once the post-graduate stage is reached, is enriched by endless academic luncheons and dinners, where high thinking is richly, yet simply and economically fed. The three dinner dishes I've chosen for January are not only some of the simplest (and most nourishing) one can eat, but each one reminds me either of the various theses on which I was working the first time I had them, or the good company I enjoyed – for university meals are just as much discussion as food.

Sausage Supreme

Serves 8
2 lb Lincolnshire or good quality sausages
2 garlic cloves, peeled and left whole
4 tbsp olive oil
1 lb winter radish, sliced
1 lb salsify, diced
½ pint dry white wine / ½ pint chicken stock
or: 1 pint chicken stock
pinch of coriander seed
½ lb mushrooms, sliced
½ lb haricot beans
2 tbsp cornflour
2 tbsp cranberry jelly or sauce
pinch of sea salt

Cut each sausage lengthways and fry with the garlic in a little oil until browned. Put in a casserole. Add the radish and salsify, then the wine and half the stock, with the coriander, mushrooms and beans. Cover, and cook at 325°F (170°C), Gas Mark 3, for 1 hour. Blend cornflour into remainder of stock, and add jelly and seasoning. Stir gently into casserole, and allow to meld for 3–4 minutes.

This can be served with baked jacket potatoes, or I prefer warm wholemeal rolls and unsalted garlic butter. It is also nice served cold the next day for luncheon.

This recipe from university days bears little resemblance to the concoctions which used to be the mainstay of Harvest suppers, and the source of village feuds for the ensuing year.

Meat and Vegetable Pie

Serves 6
3 lb lean chine or chuck steak
½ lb kidney, skinned, cored and diced
3 oz wholemeal flour, seasoned with garlic salt
3 oz butter
4 tbsp olive oil
2 garlic cloves, whole
6 oz flat mushrooms, sliced
1 pint stock
4 oz peas
4 oz carrots, sliced
½ lb Brussels sprouts
2 oz winter radish, grated
2 oz Jerusalem artichokes, diced
2 eggs
16 oz puff pastry (the frozen variety is very good)

Dice the steak and toss it and the kidney in flour. Melt the butter into half of the oil in a deep frying pan and fry meat quickly until brown. Blend in the flour, and put into casserole. Fry the garlic and mushrooms in remainder of oil, until just brown. Pour in the stock, bring to the boil and add to the meat. Add the remaining vegetables and one egg to the casserole, and cook for 2 hours at 325°F (170°C), Gas Mark 3. Drain the juices into a pan, and place the meat and vegetables in a pie dish with central funnel. Reduce juices over a fast heat, and add to meat and vegetables.

When cold, top with pastry, sealing the edges. Decorate with pastry leaves. Brush with beaten egg and bake until crispy brown at 450°F (230°C), Gas Mark 8, for 15–20 minutes.

I love this dish for its colour, as well as its goodness. Recently, it has been given the more enterprising name of Rice Maritime among our guests.

Fish and Rice

1 lb brown rice
2 tbsp olive oil
¼ pint chicken stock
2 oz butter
1 ½ oz wholemeal flour
½ pint single cream
4 oz red beans
2 oz peas
2 oz carrots, diced
4 oz Indian corn (sweet corn)
1 lb peeled prawns, drained
sea salt
parsley to garnish

In a deep pan fry the rice in oil for 5–7 minutes, stirring to separate the grains. Add the stock and simmer for 30 minutes, or until the liquid has been absorbed. Meanwhile, melt the butter, stir in the flour and cook for 3–4 minutes. Remove pan from heat and gradually add cream. Boil the vegetables for 5–7 minutes, and drain. Return sauce to the boil, stirring until it thickens. Add the prawns and vegetables to the sauce, and season. Arrange in the centre of a fish server, with an edging of rice. Garnish with parsley. For special occasions, add swirls of soured cream.

DESSERTS

The snow eventually goes and I revel in the rich greenness of the garden. The rose borders yield lemon balm and buddleia-mint leaves. Round the sundial in the sunken garden, thyme is regaining its pungency. But the lemon balm is for a recipe of my aunt's. Her prowess in the kitchen ensured 'Holm Croft', her family home, was full of children during school holidays. She died several years ago, but in the fifties and sixties this recipe was Number One in the family popularity stakes.

Auntie Betty's Flapjacks

2 oz butter
1 oz demerara sugar
2 oz honey
4 oz golden syrup
4 oz rolled oats
a few leaves of lemon balm

Grease a swiss roll tin. Mix butter, sugar, honey and syrup in a saucepan over a low heat, and stir until melted. Add oats and mix well. Line the tin with balm leaves, and press in the mixture. Bake at 350°F (180°C), Gas Mark 4, for 20–25 minutes until golden (I like mine *pale* gold). Score when warm, cut into rectangles when cold. Delicious with strong, freshly-ground coffee at any time of the day.

I'm allergic to hospital penicillin but the blue penicillium-mould in Derbyshire Blue Stilton cheese very definitely agrees with me, and is a delectable way of despatching a headache into the bargain.

For a quick, satisfying and nourishing meal, I like a generous wedge of mature Stilton with Chewy Shortcake, and strong, freshly-ground coffee.

Chewy Shortcake

6 oz wholemeal flour
5 oz sunflower margarine
3 ½ oz demerara sugar
pinch of mixed spice
small handful of caraway seed

Mix all ingredients thoroughly, and pound into round, non-stick tins. Cook at 325°F (170°C), Gas Mark 3, for 20 minutes. Score when warm, cut when cold – or serve as a shapeless, but scrumptious dessert while still hot (we call this the Wreck of the Hesperus).

Though at a sitting I eat far less than the redoubtable Parson Woodforde of two centuries ago (but perhaps he wouldn't have longed for a 20 ½ in. waist), I go along with his love of nuts. Not far from here, we have access to acres of hazeltrees, where nuts harvested in autumn see us through most years until Whitsun. Some are chopped for Pashka (see April), others go into

Demonsdale Custard

custard powder
1 pint milk
2 tbsp demerara sugar
vanilla essence
6 oz hazelnuts, chopped

Blend the amount of custard powder directed on the packet with a little cold milk until smooth. Heat remainder of milk to near-boiling. Pour on to blended powder. Return mixture to saucepan and stir to the boil. Add sugar and a few drops of vanilla essence. Stir in nuts just before serving.

BREAD AND CAKES

From the time I could stand on a chair to reach into the great yellow and brown pancheon which my mother, grandmother and great-grandmother had used, I've baked bread. At school, my Domestic Science mistress never fathomed why someone who couldn't thread a needle, could turn out quite presentable loaves. On occasion – in fact, often – I ring the changes; but my basic weekly recipe is this:

Wholemeal Bread

3 lb stoneground flour
1 tbsp sea salt or garlic salt
4 oz sunflower margarine
2 oz fresh yeast
warm water

Nowadays, I use a polythene bowl, since the pancheon was broken years ago. Shake flour lightly into a bowl. Add salt. Rub in margarine. Cream yeast in a little of the water, stir in to mixture and add sufficient water to knead to a moist dough. Flours vary in texture, so the amount of water necessary will vary also. Cover with a cloth, and set in a warm place (my favourite is a sunny windowsill) for at least 2 hours to rise.

Set oven to 425°F (220°C), Gas Mark 7. Warm three tins. Knead dough again and divide between tins. Fork lightly on top. Set tins in a warm place for 5 minutes, then place in oven and bake for 10 minutes at full heat. Turn tins through 90° and reduce heat to 375°F (190°C), Gas Mark 5, for 20–25 minutes. To test, take out a loaf; if a knock on its base sounds hollow, the bread is ready. Surplus loaves, once cooled, can be frozen. However, being 'heavy' bread, thawing-out isn't quick; you can't wait until the guests are coming up the drive.

Sterndale Sponge

4 oz butter
4 oz sugar
2 eggs
4 oz self-raising flour
a little milk
2 oz sultanas
6 scented geranium leaves

Cream butter and sugar. Add eggs with a little flour. Gradually add rest of flour and sufficient milk to mix. Fold in the fruit. Line a greased tin with geranium leaves. Bake at 400°F (200°C), Gas Mark 6, for 15–20 minutes, or until the top centre is just about to crack. Leave to cool in the tin – or, if you like, eat as a hot, if floppy, dessert.

I love Russia – the country, her people and her food, as you will see. By the time St Petersburg's morning sun peeped round the corner of Grand Duchess Yelisaveta Feodorovna's palace, to put an extra shine on the icy Nevsky Prospekt and make the crystals on the River Neva's solid ripples glitter, the temperature had risen to minus 35 °C. It rose even more one morning, when the Yevropeiskaya Hotel where I had taken a friend for a holiday caught fire. Miraculously, after the chaos which ensued, the hotel chefs dished up the most wonderful brioches I have ever tasted. One day, I've promised, I'll go back and enjoy them as they should be sampled – in the clear, crisp air of that beautiful northern city.

Brioches

8 oz strong plain flour
salt to taste
1 tbsp caster sugar
½ oz fresh yeast
a little warm water to mix
2 medium eggs
2 oz sunflower margarine

Mix flour, salt and sugar. Mix yeast into the water, and add with the beaten eggs and fat to the flour mixture. Knead, and leave to rise in a warm place for 2 hours. Heat oven to 450°F (230°C), Gas Mark 8. Re-knead, and make up into little patty-pans, with a small ball of dough off-centre on each 'bun'. Bake for 10 minutes. Eat hot, with lots of butter, and raspberry juice.

In Russia, they are served with raspberry juice in large carafes. I brought the custom back with me, but sometimes ring the changes with fresh, unsweetened strawberry or blackcurrant juice. I use the natural juices from my own frozen fruit, which is probably the nearest one can get, in the West, to the Russian juice. Tinned fruit juice is too sweet and cloying.

HERBS OF THE MONTH

Bay *Laurus nobilis*
Half-hardy evergreen, up to 20 ft but generally below 4 ft

NOT to be confused with the poisonous, shiny-leaved laurel often used in large flower-arrangements. In fact, *Laurus nobilis* is the ONLY non-poisonous member of the family.

Sacred to Apollo and used extensively in the god's temple at Delphi, it was 'inherited' by Apollo's son, *Aesculapius*. The Romans revered bay as a symbol of status and success, introducing the 'crown of laurels', from which came the baccalaureat degree and the position of poet laureate.

Even a single bay leaf can turn an ordinary Shepherd's Pie into a special dish, and every kitchen should have at least one jar of dried bay leaves. This is a herb too pungent to be used fresh. Try the leaves with all meat dishes, and with 'heavyweight' fish such as halibut and turbot. Float a leaf in liqueurs, and experiment with a snippet in custards and milk puddings. Add a leaf also when cooking Jerusalem artichokes, carrots and aubergines. Bay is a traditional ingredient of *bouquet garni*, where its companions parsley and thyme blend to give a mix of delicious fragrance.

For thousands of years bay has been valued as an antiseptic. It was used in many medicines including narcotics, for in large doses it can produce unwelcome effects. The oil extracted from bay leaves is used externally to relieve rheumatic pain, but for the amateur grower bay is valued primarily in the kitchen.

Except in favoured parts of the south-west, lean on the side of caution and grow bay in a pot or tub, overwintering in the greenhouse or home. The neat pom-pom trees of city sidewalks are less popular now than a generation ago, as we tend more to the 'natural' look. Bay is slow-growing, and your kitchen requirements may not wait for the six or seven years it takes to grow a specimen plant, so train it as an ordinary bush, gently pruning by taking out shoots as and when needed. Cuttings taken in late autumn root better with hormone rooting powder. Grow on in light, sandy soil, and protect from frost.

Sweet Violet *Viola odorata*
Hardy evergreen, to 12 in.

Due perhaps to its propensity for producing seed-heads instead of flowers as the summer advances, this herb became a symbol of fertility in the world of ancient Greece. More practically, the Romans made wine from it. Hippocrates valued it as a cure for headaches. For three millenia the rich purple flowers have flavoured desserts and drinks, and scented courts and cottages around the world. Around 1,000 BC, the sweet violet was the symbol of Athens; in the Middle Ages it was treasured by Christians as symbolizing our Lord's humility; in Britain Victoria's reign saw the heyday of 'lovely sweet violets'.

Today many acres in southern France supply this herb for the perfume industry – carrying on the popularity of a flower which was once the emblem of the Imperial Napoleonic Party in the days when the Emperor, known to his loyal supporters by the code-name 'Caporal Violette', was banished to the Isle of Elba.

The flowers can be eaten raw, or crystallized as a decoration for cakes, jellies and ice cream. Young leaves can be picked for salads, or as a last-minute garnish for soups (particularly tomato).

An infusion of the dried leaves, flowers or root can be taken to relieve bronchitis and catarrh. Fresh leaves made into a poultice take the pain from bruises. Use the root sparingly, as prolonged or excessive use can act as a purgative and emetic. Sweet violets contain Vitamin C, also violarutin, methyl salicylate and an alkaloid, odoratine. The flowers can be steeped and boiled, the resulting liquid being applied to the forehead to relieve the annoyingly common sick headache. Formerly this herb was used in the treatment of rheumatism. Oil extracted from the leaves is used in aromatherapy to treat a variety of complaints, including acne, fluid retention and respiratory disorders. It is also said to aid slimming.

Mixed with orris root, violet perfume can be used to impregnate fabrics, candles, soap and even writing-paper.

Give this herb a fairly rich, moist soil, in partial shade. Propagate from runners, or seed sown in late spring. Keep the seedlings under glass for the first year, after which they romp away. A few plants grown in an unheated greenhouse will usually give precious fragrant flowers for Christmas. Use this herb as groundcover in rosebeds and borders of spring bulbs.

Lemon Verbena *Aloysia triphylla* (also listed as *Lippia citriodora*)
Half-hardy perennial, to 3 ft

The Spaniards brought this native of Argentina and Chile to Europe. The name Aloysia commemorates Maria Louisa, queen of Charles IV of Spain, who was fond of including this lemon-scented herb in finger-bowls at her numerous and extravagant palace banquets.

Use the fresh leaves to flavour cakes, fruit salads, jams, jellies and ice cream. Try them also in vinegar, for an interesting taste with fish dishes. Young leaves are pleasant in summer drinks and salads. Lemon verbena tea is a refreshing and stimulating drink, hot or cold. From meat dishes to Christmas cakes, this herb can be used as a substitute for lemons. The finely-ground dried leaves can also be used to scent sugar. Wrap ripe tomatoes in verbena leaves for a couple of days to preserve and scent them; this also works with top fruit and courgettes.

A tea made from the dried leaves is used in the treatment of indigestion, flatulence, nausea, palpitations and bronchial congestion. However, use sparingly as the higher strength of the dried herb can produce gastric irritation.

The lemon-scented stems and foliage are useful for flower-arrangements, *pot-pourris* and sachets. The oil, comprising mainly citral, is used in the perfume industry. This herb is particularly good for scenting candles, the leaves retaining their aroma for several years: let the leaves steep in melted wax at 180°F for 45 minutes. Add verbena 'bubbles' to your bath: use 2 fl. oz glycerine, 1 fl. oz vodka and ¼ fl. oz oil of verbena.

This shrub needs winter protection in most of Britain. Ideally, grow it in a pot on the patio in summer and give it a light, not too warm, windowsill from September to Easter. Seed can be sown in heat from April to June, or beg a cutting from a friend in early summer. The fragrant leaves, not unlike those of sweet bay in shape, are the herb's glory. Its small, pale-lavender flowers are best pinched out as they appear.

Caraway *Carum carvi*
Biennial, to 2½ ft

Caraway often graced the dining table as a flavouring agent in the days of Good Queen Bess. In days of yore it was a treasured ingredient of love-potions.

The seeds form an integral part of Hungarian Goulash, but can also be used over rich meats including pork and goose, fish dishes, beetroot, potatoes, soups, rye bread, cakes, apple dishes, cheese and in bread and biscuits. They are often served in a dish of mixed seeds after a meal in India. The young leaves can be chopped into salads and soups, and used in a variety of curries. The roots can be boiled or roasted like parsnips; and the essential oil is found in several liqueurs, including Kümmel.

Safe for young and old alike, caraway seeds can be enjoyed raw or infused, to help digestion, stimulate the appetite and relieve flatulence. In the United States, caraway seeds were given to youngsters in church, to prevent them hiccuping. Today the seeds are eaten as sweets to freshen the breath: stir the seeds into egg white, then toss in icing sugar and lemon juice, and leave to harden.

Pigeon fanciers have been known to claim that if baked caraway dough is a regular part of their birds' diet, the pigeons never stray.

Caraway seed ripens about two months after flowering. When the majority of the seed looks ripe, cut the plants to the ground, and hang up the stems in a dry room over a cloth or paper to catch the seed. When dry, caraway seed lasts for months in airtight containers.

February

The rooks return —
February

He giveth snow like wool; he scattereth the
hoarfrost like ashes. He casteth forth his ice like
morsels: who can stand before his cold?
(Psalm 147:16, 17)

February

STARTERS

Cicely Chicons • Savoy Soup
• Russian Sardine Toasties •

SAVOURY LIGHT LUNCHEON/ SUPPER DISHES

Valentine Salad • Soused Mackerel
• Liver and Cheese •

DINNER (MAIN COURSE DISHES)

Spicy Rice • Parsley Schnitzel
• Convention(al) Casserole •

DESSERTS

Yorkshire Relish • Candlemas Pudding
• Herby Pancakes •

BREAD AND CAKES

Malt and Garlic Loaf • Cheesey Buns • Shrove Trifle

HERBS OF THE MONTH

Sweet Cicely • Coriander • Dill • Parsley

Except where otherwise stated, each recipe caters for four people

2 February brings the Feast of Candlemas, the Purification of the Virgin, when candles have been lit in Our Lady's honour since at least the time of Gelasius I (fifth century). Some Candlemas days are as cold and wintry as the Psalmist here describes, while others . . . I remember a beautiful mild, sunny Candlemas Sunday, when we were invited to the dedication of altar rails and lectern at St Helen's Church, Grindleford, in Derbyshire's Hope Valley. The lovely honey-coloured wood had been locally carved and given in memory of the parents of a schoolfriend of my mother's.

> *If Candlemas Day dawn fair and bright,*
> *Winter will have another flight.*

So runs the old proverb. Here, in the Derbyshire Peak District, it's a fair assumption that whatever Candlemas brings, winter will have at least another flight. Yet, when snow permits, the snowdrops demurely hang their silver bells, the rooks return to inspect their nests, crocus spears poke up in all the usual, and some unusual, places – and spring is only just round the corner.

STARTERS

Candlemas also sees the chicons – blanched shoots of chicory – at their best: in the greenhouses and local shops. So for this relatively short period we indulge in

Cicely Chicons

1 garlic clove, whole
1 oz butter
4 chicons
generous handful of sweet cicely leaves
(parsley is a good alternative)
sea salt
¼ pint chicken stock

I grow my chicons in an unheated greenhouse, but they still need a thorough rinsing to remove grit from the bases of the tightly-folded leaves. Cut off the pith, and slice lengthways. In a deep casserole lightly fry the garlic in butter. Add chicons and cicely with seasoning, and fry until golden. Remove from heat, add stock. Cover, and cook for 30–35 minutes at 350°F (180°C), Gas Mark 4.

An old gardener at the Hall here used to call the hardiest of cabbages Savoys, with a heavy Caledonian emphasis on the first syllable. With their pretty crinkled leaves and ability to come through the worst blizzards unscathed, they're worth every centimetre of ground thtey take up for so long, to the cook in winter.

Savoy Soup

1 fair-sized Savoy
1 pint chicken and garlic stock
4 fl. oz cream
1 garlic clove, whole
½ oz wholemeal flour
pinch of dill
pinch of coriander
sea salt
2 egg yolks

Shred the cabbage finely and put all the ingredients into a deep pan, gradually blending in the egg yolks last. I like to stir – not whisk – gently to the boil. Cover, and simmer gently for 35–40 minutes.

This is a really lovely, filling soup for cold days – actually a meal in itself.

Hardly a recipe at all, this is so simple – but then, one needs to save time on occasions.

Russian Sardine Toasties

Just 4 sardines and a slice of bread per person. Toast thick slices of wholemeal bread (I like malted wholemeal for this) and spread liberally with parsley butter. Top with flaked sardines and sprinkle with a suggestion of mace.

LIGHT SAVOURY DISHES

We live next to the 'Ski-run at St Moritz' in winter: that's what our postmen call the long hill down to the village, with its cute little hummock halfway down. The trick is to have a good recce at the top, and if no other vehicle is in sight, to step on the throttle and skim down. Lay-bys or passing-places are non est, *and one of two vehicles meeting has to reverse a long, long way. But the hazards during snow seem not to deter visitors, so the pantry shelves lighten even in a hard winter.*

The annoyance of late mail on 14 February usually means delays throughout the day, hence a cold luncheon. This is basically Niçoise, with our own variations.

Valentine Salad

Serves 8
3 eggs
2 lettuce or cabbage hearts, shredded
½ lb broad beans (frozen)
½ lb green runner beans (frozen)
½ lb petits pois (frozen)
2 garlic cloves, chopped not crushed
½ lb button mushrooms, washed and sliced
½ lb tomatoes
7 oz tuna or salmon, flaked
¼ pint soured cream
thyme, parsley and dill to sprinkle
2 oz landcress, for garnish

Hard-boil the eggs, leave to cool then slice. Line the salad bowl with lettuce. Cook the beans, peas, garlic and mushrooms in a little water for 7–10 minutes, and allow to cool. Slice the tomatoes, leaving the skins on – they're full of goodness. Mix the fish into half the cream. Gradually add the rest of the ingredients to the mixture and place in the salad bowl. Decorate with swirls of any remaining cream, herb butter, or just sprinkle with herbs and cress.

Mackerel used to be called 'the scavenger of the sea'. True it may be, but it puts its work to good use and presents us with a very nutritious flesh.

Soused Mackerel

Serves 6
¾ pint water
¾ pint cider vinegar
8 cloves
1 bay leaf
6 peppercorns
5 juniper berries
6 mackerel
2 garlic cloves, sliced not crushed
4 tsp mustard
2 cucumbers in dill*
6 large cabbage leaves
cornflour

Simmer ¾ pint of water, the vinegar, cloves, bay leaf, peppercorns and juniper for 10–15 minutes, and allow to cool.

Gut the mackerel, keeping the heads and tails for stock. Wash, and dry. Open the body and spread with garlic, mustard and cucumber slices. Roll each fish in a cabbage leaf, secure with a skewer. Lay in a baking dish. Thicken the juniper marinade with a little cornflour, and pour over the fish. Cover with foil and bake for 20–25 minutes at 350°F (180°C), Gas Mark 4.

My mackerel are left to souse for two days on a stone bench in the bottom pantry, but a fridge works just as well. I like to serve them on hot buttered rye bread.

*Cucumbers-in-dill

8 small cucumbers (pickling cucumbers)
2 oz sea salt
handful of fresh dill
1 tsp dill seeds
1 tsp coriander seeds
1 tsp black peppercorns (optional)
3 ½ fl. oz white wine vinegar

Slice cucumbers and chop dill into a 3 ½ pint jar. Into a saucepan pour 2 pints water. Add salt, dill and coriander seeds, peppercorns and vinegar. Boil for 3 minutes from cold. When cooled, pour over cucumbers and dill. Seal jar and store for 3–4 weeks in a cool, dark place.

This now-favourite dish grew out of necessity – though it's perhaps a strange breadline that has only pig's liver and Stilton cheese in the pantry! But it happened in 1982, after a snowbound four weeks.

Liver and Cheese

2 lb pig's liver, sliced
sunflower margarine
wholewheat bread
garlic butter
½ lb Derbyshire Blue Stilton
rosemary

Grill the liver in a little margarine, until lightly sealed on both sides. Toast rounds of bread, and spread with garlic butter. Arrange liver slices on the bread. Top with slivers of Stilton. Grill gently until cheese begins to bubble/brown. Sprinkle with rosemary and serve.

MAIN COURSE DISHES

Collecting rocks, minerals and fossils always seemed less gruesome than suffocating butterflies and sticking them on pins, or furthering the countryside's demise by picking wild flowers. The stone trail led to Anglesey, with its rich geological history. On the way we stopped at Conway, parked the car with its front wheels perilously near the water at the edge of the quay, and sampled a recipe which was to become a firm favourite. One day, I'll return – the cafe may still be there.

Spicy Rice

Serves 6
8 oz brown rice
2 oz butter
½ tsp ground ginger
½ tsp ground coriander
½ tsp ground fenugreek
2 garlic cloves, whole
¼ tsp chilli powder
1 tbsp sesame seeds
½ pint soured cream
4 oz flat mushrooms, sliced
½ oz red beans
¾ pint chicken and garlic stock
1 ½ tsp olive oil
sea salt

Boil the rice in 3 pints of salted water, until all the water is absorbed. Stir in the rest of the ingredients, return to the boil, then simmer for 15–20 minutes.

After this, I can put in several hours' hard climbing for geological specimens. You may like this dish hot: I prefer it cold.

Parsley Schnitzel

Serves 8
2 lb beef, ⅛ in. sirloin thinly sliced
2 oz wholemeal flour
sea salt
2 eggs
8 oz wholemeal breadcrumbs
4 oz parsley butter
4 tbsp olive oil
2 cloves garlic, whole
1 lemon, sliced
12 fresh parsley sprigs

Coat each slice of beef in seasoned flour. Beat eggs well, and brush or dip slices. Roll in breadcrumbs. In a deep pan heat butter, olive oil and garlic. Fry meat quickly, 4–5 minutes a side. Drain, and garnish with lemon and parsley.

I love this dish with Duchesse potatoes – creamed potatoes, with beaten egg, piped into cones and baked at 400°F (200°C), Gas Mark 6, for 20 minutes – and roasted parsnips.

I was introduced to this casserole at one of those midweek ecclesiastical conventions which must see hundreds of delegates serving up similar dishes the next weekend! I've not copied it in toto – the herbal variations are homegrown.

Convention(al) Casserole

Serves 6
6 lamb hearts or 3 lb pigs liver
juice of 1 lemon
3 tbsp wholemeal flour
2 oz butter
2 garlic cloves, chopped not crushed
salt and pepper to taste
2 bay leaves
½ pint cider
½ tsp dill
2 large cooking apples, sliced
1 tsp demerara sugar
1½ tsp ground coriander

Slice the meat into ½ in. strips, discarding the fat. Steep in lemon juice for 30 minutes. Dry with absorbent paper and roll in flour. Fry them quickly in butter in a deep casserole. Add garlic, and fry until brown. Season, and add bay leaves, cider and dill. Cover meat with slices of apple, and sprinkle with sugar and coriander. Cover with a lid and cook gently at 300°F (150°C), Gas Mark 2, for 1–1¼ hours. Delicious with chipped potatoes or mashed potatoes with parsley butter.

DESSERTS

My mother always preferred sweet to savoury dishes, and these predominate in her 'Book of Receipts', according to which this relish has been enjoyed by our family for 150 years.

Yorkshire Relish

½ lb white flour
¼ lb sugar
¼ lb jam (I like raspberry)
¼ pint milk
¼ lb suet
1 tsp bicarbonate of soda

Mix all ingredients well, adding the bicarbonate last. Place in a greased mould and steam for 2 ½ hours. Serve with ice cream.

This recipe's so good we celebrate Candlemas long after 2 February!

Candlemas Pudding

Serves 6
3 tbsp black treacle
6 oz demerara sugar
4 oz sunflower margarine
2 eggs, beaten
6 oz self-raising flour
2 tbsp cream
2 medium cooking apples, sliced
3 oz sultanas
¼ oz shredded balm leaves
¾ oz lavender butter (butter impregnated with a few lavender leaves)

Pour the treacle into a pudding basin. Cream the sugar and margarine and beat in the eggs, flour and cream. Mix the apples with the remaining ingredients, and add alternate layers of pudding mix and fruit to the treacle. Cover, and steam for 2–2 ½ hours.

While the men of Ashbourne, 20 miles from here, are preparing to get thoroughly wet at their Shrovetide football match, I prepare the day before, to enjoy these

Herby Pancakes

4 oz malted wholemeal flour or
ordinary wholemeal
sea salt
1 egg, lightly beaten
½ pint milk
pinch each of lemon verbena,
lavender, mint and dill
margarine

Mix flour and salt. With a wooden spoon make a hollow in the centre, and add the beaten egg. Add half the milk gradually, and beat well. Let it rest for 30 minutes, and add remaining milk, beating until smooth. Allow to stand for 24 hours.

Just before cooking, add pinches of lemon verbena, lavender, mint and dill. Using a small amount of margarine only to prevent sticking, fry quickly in a hot, shallow pan, browning on both sides. Eat hot, with butter and caster sugar.

BREAD AND CAKES

I've made bread for as long as I can remember, and I'm still experimenting with new flours, new herbs, new methods. Bread is wonderfully original: no two efforts ever turn out quite the same.

Malt and Garlic Loaf

1 ½ oz fresh yeast
warm water
3 lb malted wholemeal flour
sea salt
6 oz sunflower margarine
2 garlic cloves, chopped
pinch of caraway

Crumble the yeast into the water until it bubbles. Put flour into a plastic mixing bowl. Mix in salt and rub in fat. Add garlic and caraway. Pour in the yeast and mix thoroughly. Cover bowl with a cloth and leave in a warm place overnight.

Take out dough, knead thoroughly and shape into cobs or place in tins. Place on warm grill shelf while oven heats to 425°F (220°C), Gas Mark 7. Cook for 10 minutes, then turn the loaves by 90 degrees and reduce heat to 375°F (190°C), Gas Mark 5, and cook for a further 30–35 minutes, until the loaves sound hollow when knocked.

The trouble with these is they vanish between meals!

Cheesey Buns

Makes 12
7 oz self-raising flour
1 oz ground rice
3 oz demerara sugar
sea salt
3 oz sunflower margarine
½ cheese, grated (Wensleydale is my favourite)
1 egg
1 tbsp cream

Mix flour and ground rice, sugar and salt in a bowl. Add small pieces of margarine and rub in well. Add grated cheese. Beat egg into cream, and add to dry mixture. Stir in gently. Form mixture into balls and bake in bun cases, or little tins, at 425°F (220°C), Gas Mark 7, for 10–15 minutes.

Cooked in a sponge tin, this makes a super hot dessert, served with lavender custard – ordinary custard, decorated with a few dried lavender flowers on top. Piquant, exquisite, and different!

Not to be served to drivers, or to be enjoyed during the penitential six and a half weeks of Lent!

Shrove Trifle

Serves 8
1½ pints vanilla custard*
3 oz demerara sugar
½ pint white wine
1½ lb peaches, sliced (tinned or frozen)
10 sponge cubes or 5 sponge fingers
5 fl oz brandy
½ pint double cream
candied angelica

Make the custard and leave to cool. In a pan, bring sugar and wine to the boil. Add the peaches when all sugar has dissolved. Leave to cool. In a trifle dish, arrange the sponge cubes. Pour in the peaches, syrup and brandy. Gently add the custard, and leave to chill (or put in the fridge for 1½–2 hours). Swirl the cream over the custard just before serving, and decorate with angelica.

*Vanilla Custard

4½ oz caster sugar
4 eggs
1 pint milk
¼ pint water
2–3 drops vanilla essence

Warm milk and water in a pan. Beat eggs in basin and add sugar. Add to milk and stir over fairly low heat till smooth. Add vanilla and leave to cool.

HERBS OF THE MONTH

Sweet Cicely *Myrrhis odorata,* 'British Myrrh'
Hardy perennial, to 2 ½ ft

Some authorities believe this is a native of Britain, but another of its common names, 'Roman Plant', suggests a more southerly origin. In Roman gardens it was planted to attract bees. The Greeks prized it for its scent (hence the name). Later, it was dedicated to St Cecilia – perhaps because it was found that, mixed with angelica, it warded off the plague. Dioscorides had called it 'Seseli', a name which stuck until the sixteenth century, later being known affectionately as 'Sweet Cis'.

The herbalist Gerard maintained that its boiled roots, added to salad and dressed with oil and vinegar, were 'very good for old people that are dull and without courage'. Take heart and take myrrh! He also says, quaintly: 'It is used very much among the Dutch people in a kinde of loblolly or hotchpot which they do eat, called Warmus.' Culpeper, while extolling its virtues as an antidote to plague, says generously: 'It is so harmless, you cannot use it amiss.'

Sweet cicely has a pleasant, aniseed flavour. The stems can be candied like angelica. Chop young leaves for salads and cream cheese. Sprinkle on omelettes and summer fruit. Avoid using in highly seasoned dishes, which overlay sweet cecily's delicate aroma. However, when cooked with cabbage, it annuls the brassica smell. Cook the stems with tart fruit to give natural sweetening; diabetics can use this herb as a sugar substitute. Boil the roots and serve as an entree with a mild cheese sauce. Sweet cicely is used to flavour some liqueurs, notably Chartreuse, and the root can be added to brandy for an interesting flavour.

It's pleasant to chew the seed, whether or not one wants to cure indigestion. Use an infusion of the crushed seeds or leaves to ease flatulence, stimulate the appetite and clear the bronchial tubes. In the seventeenth century, the ground seed was mixed with beeswax and used as a furniture polish, still as effective today.

Give sweet cicely moist soil, in sun or partial shade. It self-sows freely, once introduced to the garden. The attractive feathery leaves are bright green, and the white umbels of flowers ripen to long black seeds. Sow the seeds in autumn, for they need to be chilled to break dormancy. This is one of the earliest plants to grow in the spring, and one of the last to die down in the autumn.

Coriander *Coriandrum sativum*
Annual, to 2 ½ ft

We know that coriander has been valued in cultivation for thousands of years. It is likely that the Romans introduced it to Britain. In Tudor times it was one of the ingredients of Hippocras, a drink popular at weddings.

The seeds have a spicy flavour when dried. Stored in airtight containers, the flavour improves with keeping. For culinary purposes, always crush or pound the dried seeds before use.

Coriander enlivens curry powder and mixed spice, tomato chutney, Ratatouille, soups, sauces, many vegetable dishes, apple pies, cakes and biscuits. Coat whole seeds with sugar, and add to homemade marmalade. Fresh young leaves can be added to curries, sauces, stews and salads. The stem can be cooked in soups and with beans, and removed before serving. Even the root can be scrubbed, chopped roughly and cooked as a vegetable in its own right, or added to curries.

In ancient times coriander was regarded as an aphrodisiac. When eaten or drunk to excess, it can act as a narcotic. Today its agreeable flavour is used to make some medicines more palatable. Its oil is added to ointments for treating rheumatism. Merely chewing the seeds does the digestion a power of good, and acts as a mild sedative; or the seeds can be infused as a pleasant-tasting tea, with the same results.

Earmark a sunny, well-drained part of your garden for this obliging annual, and grow at least a thimbleful of seed each year, to spice your diet.

Dill *Anethum graveolens*
Hardy annual, to 2 ft

In Ancient Greece, Dioscorides knew that dill 'stayeth the hickets'; and the Egyptians proffered it to guests who had succumbed to 'gippy tummy'. This Mediterranean herb was introduced to Britain by the Romans and some seeds have been found in the remains at Silchester. In the Middle Ages, while magicians flirted with dill in various spells, the common people rather more practically discovered it acted as an aphrodisiac in wine. It became known as 'Meeting-House Seed' in North America, where young and old among the early settlers found it pleasant to chew during the over-long sermons.

Today, the seeds are used mainly for flavouring cakes, but are also tasty (whole or crushed) in fish dishes, pickles and soups. Cooked with cabbage, they annul the smell. Press them into butter, and add a few when baking bread (used together with caraway seeds, the bread tastes even better). Use the young leaves and stems as you would the seeds but more sparingly, for you'll want some seeds to harvest at the end of the season. In Scandinavia dill leaves are used as we use mint, when cooking peas and new potatoes. For pickling cucumbers, dill vinegar is essential: steep the dill seeds in vinegar for two or three days, until the flavour is as strong as you wish.

Oil of dill is used in a number of over-the-counter medicines for digestive ills. Use it as Dill Water (8 drops to 1 pint distilled water); dose: one to four teaspoonfuls. Alternatively, take 2–3 drops on a sugar lump. A home-brewed mild infusion of dill seeds has a significantly beneficial and soothing effect on the digestion, or simply nibble a pinch of seeds at the end of a rich meal to achieve similar results.

Sow the seed in April, either in pots or the open ground. Contrary to some growers, I've never had trouble in trans-planting dill seedlings. The threadlike leaves are more delicate than those of fennel. The yellow flowers are produced in generous umbels. Cut the old flower stems just ahead of the seed ripening or you'll forfeit a lot to the wind. Hang the stems in a warm, dry place, with trays underneath to catch the crop. Store the seeds in airtight jars for the winter.

Parsley *Petroselinum crispum*
Short-lived perennial, to 10 in.

Introduced to Britain 400 years ago from southern Europe, parsley has been known and used from Roman times. According to Pliny, the Romans considered no sauce or salad complete without parsley. Its evergreen habit (in some years it's a biennial, but mostly a short-lived perennial) encouraged use at funerals, to denote belief in the ongoing life of the soul.

Used fresh, a nibble of parsley takes the smell of garlic off the breath, and does the digestion good at the same time. It's rich in Vitamins A, B and C, so grow a lot and use with a generous hand.

In the kitchen, parsley's uses are legion. Add it fresh or dried to soups, stews and sauces. Incorporate it in any fish dish. Use it fresh in salads, egg dishes and with all potato recipes. Roots of 'Hamburg' parsley are delicious boiled like parsnips, shredded into soups and stews, or grated raw into salads. A brown bread and parsley sandwich is good to eat after a dish of Jerusalem artichokes: flatulence induced by the latter is remedied by the parsley. Infuse some fresh leaves, and use the cold lotion as a skin tonic. In some cases, freckles will respond to this treatment.

The Greek *petros selinon* means 'Rock Celery', but in the garden parsley does best on good, deeply cultivated soil. There are three basic sorts: the Hamburg, or turnip-rooted parsley, in which the swollen underground stem is used like parsnips; the French, or smooth-leaved, sometimes known as Neapolitan; and the one most commonly grown in Britain, with tightly-curled leaves. Legend has it that parsley goes to the Devil and back seven times, before growing. Certainly the seeds are slow to germinate, taking around 28 days. Some growers try to hasten germination by pouring hot water over the seeds, but I've never found this to work. Parsley is one of the few herbs which must be dried *quickly*. Use the heat of an oven that's just cooked bread or a roast, for economy.

March

Simnel Cake —
March.

God so loved the world, that he gave his only-
begotten Son, that whosoever believeth in him,
would not perish but have everlasting life.
(John 3:16)

March

STARTERS

Spinach Eggs • Leek and Horseradish Soup
• Halibut Fingers •

SAVOURY LIGHT LUNCHEON/ SUPPER DISHES

Chicken Simples • Gribyi Po-Russky
• Salmon aux Herbes •

DINNER (MAIN COURSE DISHES)

Spring Loaf • Kedgeree • Fidgety Pie

DESSERTS

Simnel Cake • Lenten Pudding • Sultana Custard

BREAD AND CAKES

Soda Loaf • Orange Cake • Blackberry Rock Buns

HERBS OF THE MONTH

Horseradish • Salad Burnet • Rue • French Tarragon

Except where otherwise stated, each recipe caters for four people

Lent is a time for setting aside some portion of each day, over and above the hours we spend at worship or Bible study, to try to understand more of the love that made such a verse as John 3:16 possible. It's one of the greatest challenges in life, because we know we cannot *fully understand God's love* – but that's a poor reason for not trying.

March is the month when the first annual vegetable and herb seeds are sown, full of promise for the season ahead. It's also a favourite time for retreats. One year I went on two retreats, in two consecutive weeks of March. I hope my soul gained something. I know my waistline did – and it takes an awful lot of food to expand a midriff which has stood at 20½ in. for nearly half a century. Most of this month's recipes first tickled my taste-buds at other vicarages and rectories – and none the worse for that.

STARTERS

Spinach Eggs

Serves 6 (or more, if a big meal follows)
½ lb spinach, fresh if possible
1 oz tarragon, chopped or dried
3 oz soft curd cheese
1 oz Parmesan cheese, grated
12 eggs, hard-boiled
6 egg yolks, hard-boiled
pinch of nutmeg
salt and pepper to taste

Chop spinach fairly fine. Cook for 5–7 minutes. Drain. Chop tarragon (I prefer the Russian over the French) and mix with spinach into the cheeses. Mix in the 6 chopped egg-yolks. Pound well, adding nutmeg. Cut the 12 whole eggs lengthways, and arrange mixture between halves (i.e. in the manner of a banana split). Use the remaining egg-whites either as a basis for a herby sandwich-spread, or add them to the stockpot.

For a day when the temperature allows deep digging try

Leek and Horseradish Soup

Serves 6
6 leeks
4 oz sliced flat mushrooms
6 peppercorns
1 clove garlic, chopped
1 oz horseradish root, grated
½ pint single cream
5 fl. oz natural or nut yoghurt
2 tbsp tarragon vinegar
1 oz sultanas
pinch of rue
salt and pepper to taste

Wash leeks and chop finely. Cook in a very little water with the mushrooms, peppercorns, garlic and horseradish. Stir in the cream and yoghurt. Add vinegar and sultanas. Season, and serve either hot or cold.

There has to be an 'instant' recipe, even in Lent!

Halibut Fingers

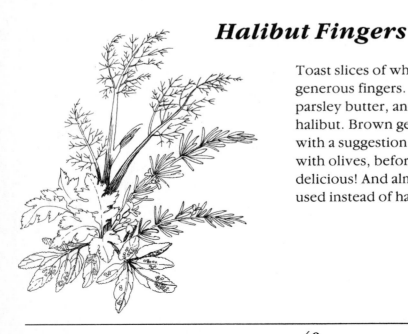

Toast slices of wholemeal bread and cut into generous fingers. Spread generously with parsley butter, and top with cooked, flaked halibut. Brown gently under the grill. Sprinkle with a suggestion of lemon juice and decorate with olives, before serving. So simple, so delicious! And almost as good if cod or hake is used instead of halibut.

LIGHT SAVOURY DISHES

The year was 1977, our Queen's Jubilee Year. However, that March our date was with HM Queen Elizabeth the Queen Mother, then Chancellor of London University, at the Royal Albert Hall. It was a day of great excitement, gowns, mortarboards and variously-coloured hoods; a day when the Albert Memorial photo-session resembled a rookery of ungainly flapping, after the decorum of the degree ceremony; a day when we were introduced to Chicken Simples.

At least, that's what we've come to call them. Today my recipe bears little resemblance to the original version. I'm always modifying this dish, according to the herbs to hand – which I think gives it extra appeal.

Chicken Simples

Serves 6
2 tbsp olive oil
1 tsp fenugreek
1 tsp coriander
1 tsp cumin
12 cardamom seeds, husked
½ in. cube ginger, grated
¼ tsp turmeric
4 tsp garam masala
1 tsp alfalfa seed
8 garlic cloves, whole (if you don't love garlic as I do, reduce to 2)
6 chicken breasts
½ oz tarragon, dried or 12 fresh sprigs
salt and pepper
¼ pint chicken and garlic stock
6 evenly-sized potatoes
garlic butter

Heat the oil in a deep pan and fry the spices for 2–3 minutes. Add the garlic cloves, and fry until nearly brown. Slice the chicken and add to the pan, cooking quickly until golden brown. Add the tarragon, seasoning and stock. Stir in well. Cover, and simmer for 1 hour. In a pre-heated oven, meanwhile, bake the scrubbed and pricked potatoes at 400°F (200°C), Gas Mark 6, for 1 hour. To serve, halve each potato lengthways (not quite cutting right through the lower edge), and pack with the simples. Top with a knob of garlic butter.

Please don't slavishly follow this herb mix; have fun with variations! For instance, a less spicy mix could include marjoram, parsley and thyme.

They say you've not been to Russia if you haven't picked
mushrooms in her massive forests and rolling grasslands.
Certainly we ate a great variety when we were there. Families
take boxes, bags and baskets into the countryside, and then
string their bounty in the autumn sun, or over a warm stove,
to dry for the winter. We haven't (or, rather, we don't make use
of) such a wide variety of fungi in Britain, so make Gribyi with
the ubiquitous field mushroom (flavoursome flats, if possible;
buttons, if necessary).

Gribyi Po-Russky

Serves 8
1 ½ lb mushrooms
2 garlic cloves, chopped
pinch of horseradish, grated
1 oz sunflower margarine
16 thin streaky bacon rashers
1 tsp burnet or cicely
pinch of rue or parsley
½ pint soured cream
8 slices wholemeal toast, buttered
salt to taste
lemon juice

Gently fry the mushrooms, garlic and
horseradish in the margarine. In another pan,
fry bacon with no added fat until crispy.
Drain, and break or chop into slivers. Stir
herbs into the soured cream. Gradually add
the bacon and mushrooms into the cream, and
season. Heat gently to eating temperature, and
serve on toast with a suggestion of lemon.

This began life here as a birthday celebration which needed to
be light, as an elaborate dinner was to be enjoyed in the evening.
It's handy for that quick luncheon which you nevertheless want
your guests to remember with pleasure.

Salmon aux Herbes

Serves 6
9 oz butter
6 slices of toasting wholemeal bread
7 eggs
3 tbsp double cream
pinches of tarragon, parsley and basil
salt and pepper to taste
¼ lb smoked salmon pieces, chopped
1 leek, sliced
2 tomatoes, thinly sliced

In a sauté pan melt half the butter. Steep the bread in it and heat until crisp in a 400°F (200°C), Gas Mark 6 oven, for 15–20 minutes. Set aside and keep warm. Lightly beat the eggs and blend in the cream, herbs, seasoning and fish. Gently melt the remainder of the butter in a deep pan and fry the leeks. Add the egg and fish mixture to the pan, stir slowly until the eggs begin to curdle. Serve piping hot on the toast, decorated with wafer-thin tomato slices.

MAIN COURSE DISHES

Dinners in Lent, while I don't exclude meat, are lighter than normal. As well as believing moderation is more in line with our Lord's wilderness experience, cutting back on one's intake is also yet another way of marking Lent. I'm sure Easter has a greater significance as a result.

Spring Loaf

Serves 4–6
2 cloves garlic, chopped
1 tbsp olive oil
2 tsp Bovril
4 tbsp chicken stock
3 oz nuts, chopped
3 oz sultanas
6 oz brown rice
1 egg
pinches of mint and tarragon
suggestion of rue
salt and pepper
For the stuffing:
8 oz spinach, pounded
3 oz parsnips, finely sliced
3 oz carrots, finely sliced
3 oz Derby or Cheddar cheese, grated

Fry garlic in oil until translucent. Heat Bovril and stock, and blend in nuts, sultanas, fried garlic and rice. Beat in egg, and add herbs and seasoning.

Grease or use a non-stick 2 lb loaf tin. Divide mixture into four. Press one part of the rice mixture into the bottom of the tin. Add a layer of spinach. Top with the next rice layer, followed by parsnips and carrots. On top of the third rice layer, the cheese. Finish with the remaining rice mix. Press down well. Cook at 400°F (200°C), Gas Mark 6, for 25–30 minutes. Serve with a seasonal green salad, or on a bed of tangy watercress.

My variations on the original may not be recognized in Bombay or Delhi, but then a Derbyshire garden grows different spices.

Kedgeree

8 oz brown rice
milk
3 eggs
12 oz cod
2 garlic cloves, chopped
3 oz butter
½ tsp cumin
½ tsp coriander
¼ tsp turmeric
sea salt
3 tbsp soured cream
parsley to garnish

Cook rice in 3 pints of milk for 20 minutes. Hard-boil the eggs and set aside to cool. Gently poach fish in a very little milk. Drain, and allow to cool. Fry the garlic in half of the butter until slightly brown. Flake cod, shell and slice eggs. Add both to pan with rice and remainder of the butter. Stir gently and heat well through. Add spices and seasoning and a little cream. Heat up again. Garnish with parsley and cream, and serve on large shells (either real shells or heatproof polythene ones), for a special welcome.

The first time I made this pie the dough turned out so pernickety, I sympathized with the chef who named it. My vocation is not to construct elaborately-artistic pastry designs – but the rare occasions when the results are reasonable encourage me to dish this pie up again and again. A Lenten penance? Perhaps, but it tastes a treat.

Fidgety Pie

Serves 6
8 rashers streaky bacon
8 oz herby sausage meat
1 large cooking apple, sliced
1 lb waxy potatoes (floury ones fall apart), sliced
2 garlic cloves, chopped
2 tsp demerara sugar
¼ oz each of dried mint, tarragon and chives
sea salt and pepper to taste
½ pint chicken stock
Pastry:
3 oz butter
5 oz wholemeal flour
salt
milk to mix and glaze

Chop bacon and sausage-meat and place in a 1 ½ pint pie dish. Layer thin slices of apple and potato on top. Chop garlic and sprinkle over slices. Add sugar, herbs and seasoning to stock, and pour gently on.

Set oven to 350°F (180°C), Gas Mark 4. Rub fat into flour and a little salt to make crumbs. Mix with milk or water into a stiff dough. Roll out and cut to form a lid on the pie dish. Then try to be artistic with the bits left over! Glaze with milk. Bake for 1 ½ hours and serve hot with leeks or Jerusalem artichokes.

DESSERTS

The Fourth Sunday in Lent is Mothering Sunday, when traditional Simnel Cake is obligatory – though how authentically-traditional this is by now is open to question. In fact, many eat it at Easter.

Simnel Cake

½ lb butter
½ lb demerara sugar
4 large eggs
Peel of 2 oranges
6 oz nuts, chopped
2 lb sultanas or 1 lb each currants and sultanas
pinch of baking powder
salt to taste
½ tsp nutmeg
½ tsp cumin
14 oz strong plain flour
milk to mix
Topping:
4 oz ground almonds
4 oz icing sugar
4 oz caster sugar
1 egg
4 lemon geranium leaves, chopped
lemon juice

Cream butter and sugar. Beat in eggs and blend in orange peel, finely chopped, and nuts. Mix baking powder, salt and spices into flour, and add gradually to fruit mixture. Mix if necessary with a little milk. Spoon the mixture into a lined and greased 7 in. cake tin. Bake at 350°F (180°C), Gas Mark 4, for 3–3 ½ hours.

Blend ground almonds and sugar. Add beaten egg and lemon leaves and juice. Work like dough until smooth. Top the cake with a generous layer of icing (the sides are usually tied round with yellow ribbon), and roll the remainder of the paste into balls. Place round the top of the cake, giving a 'crown' appearance. Fluffy yellow chicks are Easter additions!

For a hot dessert try

Lenten Pudding

Serves 4–6
6 oz self-raising flour
1 tsp baking powder
pinch of salt
4 oz beef suet, shredded
4 oz demerara sugar
3 oz fresh white breadcrumbs
1 egg
milk to mix
1 lb apricot halves (tinned)

Lightness is the keynote, so I slowly sift the flour, baking powder and a pinch of salt into the mixing bowl. Add suet, sugar and breadcrumbs, and mix thoroughly. Stir in beaten egg and milk to mix. Blend in apricot halves, keeping four halves back to line the bottom of a 2 pint pudding basin. Spoon in the mixture, cover with a folded piece of greaseproof paper, fluted to allow for expansion. Tie the paper securely on.

Place basin in a steamer over a pan half-filled with simmering water. Cover with a tight-fitting lid and steam for 2 ½ hours, keeping the water level topped up as evaporation occurs. Turn the pudding on to a hot dish to serve, and enjoy it with apricot honey in lieu of custard.

I prefer my custards as desserts in their own right, like this one my mother used to make far better than I've ever managed.

Sultana Custard

1 pint milk
2 tbsp demerara sugar
2 tbsp golden syrup
4 egg yolks
3 oz sultanas
pinch of nutmeg and lemon balm

Heat the milk in a pan almost to boiling. Stir in sugar and syrup. Beat egg yolks well and add to milk. Stir until creamy. Add sultanas. Remove from heat and allow to cool slightly. Serve in sundae dishes and sprinkle with nutmeg and balm.

BREAD AND CAKES

---

*I'm still intrigued by reactions from around the retreat refectory
tables when fellow-diners discover someone who bakes her own
bread. Usually it's a case of: 'Oh, Mother used to', or 'I did – when
I had more time.' A friend who's a nun commented: 'One of our
community fancies herself as a bread-maker.' Poor soul, it
sounded as though she'd be doing all the convent bread for a
long time to come.*

I love soda bread. It's unique – and quick!

Soda Loaf

For 3 loaves:
1 ½ lb strong plain flour
1 ½ lb wholemeal flour
3 tsp bicarbonate of soda
sea salt
½ oz caraway seeds
6 ½ oz sunflower margarine
1 ½ pints buttermilk (or milk)[1]

In a plastic[2] bowl mix flours, soda, salt and caraway seeds. Rub in fat. Add buttermilk and mix to a pliant dough, if necessary adding a little warm water. After a light kneading, shape into cobs and allow to stand for 5 minutes on greased baking trays in a warm place. Prick or score the top of each loaf. Bake at 400°F (200°C), Gas Mark 6, for 30–35 minutes. Delicious eaten hot with honey.

---

[1] Buttermilk, which is what remains after butter is extracted, can usually be obtained from the larger health food shops.
[2] I always use plastic (polythene) bowls for breadmaking, ensuring no chilling of the flour from the outset.

My mother couldn't eat lemons, and the habit of preferring oranges has stuck with me. This cake recipe, however, takes equally kindly to lemons.

Orange Cake

6 oz sunflower margarine
6 oz demerara sugar
juice and grated rind of 1 orange or lemon
3 eggs, beaten
6 oz self-raising flour
6 oz muesli
¼ pint milk
½ tsp allspice
3 drops vanilla essence

Cream fat and sugar. Add orange rind and blend in beaten eggs, flour, muesli, milk, spice, vanilla and juice. Mix thoroughly. Spoon into a lined and greased 7 in. cake tin. Bake at 350°F (180°C), Gas Mark 4, for 50–60 minutes. Eat hot or cold.

By now the blackberries spared at Christmas are almost all gone, but I can usually find a bag or two somewhere in the freezer. Tinned or frozen raspberries or strawberries are – almost – as delicious for

Blackberry Rock Buns

Makes 12 buns
8 oz wholemeal flour
pinch of salt
2 tsp baking powder
4 oz sunflower margarine
6 oz blackberries
4½ oz demerara sugar
1 large egg
milk to mix
12 scented geranium leaves

Mix flour, salt and baking powder in a bowl. Rub in fat to make a crumbly texture. Mix in berries and sugar. Beat in egg and mix if necessary with milk, but keep a stiff texture. Place a geranium leaf in each of 12 bun cases, and top with the mixture. Bake at 400°F (200°C), Gas Mark 6, for 15–20 minutes. A nice nibble for supper, with coffee or hot chocolate.

HERBS OF THE MONTH

Horseradish *Cochlearia armoracia* (Syn. *Armoracia rusticana*)
Hardy perennial, 2–3 ft

Horseradish has been appreciated in Scandinavia and Germany for many centuries. In Britain we cottoned on to its virtues only in the mid-seventeenth century – and even then, as a purely medicinal herb.

Today, its culinary properties are best enjoyed as a sauce accompanying meat and fish dishes, and as a relish for salads. The young leaves add zest to salads, but use sparingly.

Prolonged winter frosts can lock the roots in cold storage, so in autumn lift some thongs, wash thoroughly, slice thinly and dry in a low oven heat, or on a sunny windowsill. Store in airtight jars. Alternatively, slice, freeze on open trays, and then pack in freezer bags.

A whiff of horseradish acts like smelling-salts, makes short work of sinus blockages, and reduces to tears those whose job it is to grate the roots for the kitchen. Horseradish contains Vitamin C, calcium, sodium and magnesium: it aids the digestion and stimulates the appetite. It has antibiotic qualities, but can react adversely on certain skins and inflame the gastro-intestinal mucosae.

Grow horseradish alongside potato rows, to prevent disease attacking the tubers; and either plant near fruit trees, or use a diluted infusion of the grated root to spray against brown rot in apples.

Horseradish is a vigorous and uncomplaining grower, but can be exterminated by over-zealous using of the roots. Give it a good rich soil, not too much sun, and plenty of room. Beg root-cuttings (thongs) from a friend in late spring or autumn, and plant with tears in your eyes and hope in your heart.

Salad Burnet *Poterium sanguisorba* (Syn. *Sanguisorba minor*)
Perennial, to 8 in.

The name Sanguisorba is thought to derive from the styptic properties of the roots. Salad burnet was among the herbs taken to New England by the Pilgrim Fathers. The flowers, like tiny red oval-shaped drumheads, contain no nectar, and are dependent on the wind for pollination. Garden alleyways in Tudor times were planted with the fragrant triumvirate of chamomile, burnet and thyme.

Use the leaves to give a cucumber-like, slightly nutty flavour to cream cheese, salads, herb butters and garnishes. Burnet is one of the few herbs which is best added at the *beginning* of cooking, to vegetables, casseroles and soups. Use this sauce with white fish: 2 tbsp burnet, 2 tbsp tarragon or mint, 4 oz melted butter. Simmer for 15 minutes. Burnet combines well with rosemary, when cooking meat. It can also be used to flavour vinegar and a variety of salad dressings, and makes cool summer drinks cooler (used with, or without, borage).

Burnet leaves are quite rich in Vitamin C, and as a tea have diuretic and tonic properties. Almost evergreen, they can be picked fresh for most of the year. Dried and infused, they are useful for many blood disorders, skin problems, even sunburn – given the odd British heatwave, or mis-timed holiday!

If you run out of ideas for Christmas or birthday presents, lightly melt some candles, and press dried burnet leaves into the sides. Experiment with other dried herbs: candles of mixed fragrances are particularly effective.

Grow Salad Burnet in a sunny position near the edge of the border, for easy picking. It appreciates lime in the soil. Seeds sown in late spring will give pickings by July, and usually self-sow readily if the plants are allowed to flower. This herb is sometimes slow to re-start in the spring, so be careful not to disturb the dormant crowns when weeding.

Rue *Ruta graveolens*
Fairly hardy perennial, small bush to 2 ½ ft

Rue has had a variety of uses. Mithridates employed it as an antidote to several poisons. For centuries, after the Chinese had explored its medicinal properties, it was used to treat various eye complaints: Michelangelo and Leonardo da Vinci were among its adherents. Infuse the leaves, and bathe the eyes when the liquid has cooled. The Romans introduced it to Britain, but modern trends have largely allowed its possibilities to lapse unexploited. Rue sprigs were used as the aspergillum, to sprinkle holy water at Mass – a practice which is probably responsible for its common name 'Herb of Grace'.

It can be used in the kitchen, but very sparingly; I particularly like a snippet with cream cheese and homemade brown bread.

A natural insect-repellent, it imparts a fresh smell reminiscent of bitter almonds to clothes in cupboards and drawers. I like to sleep with a sprig under my pillow. For our annual Church Flower Festival I strew fresh rue in the porch each day, to give a delightful scent, and to deter insects from entering the church and pollinating the flowers. Rue is tough, and withstands a lot of treading.

In the garden, give it a position in full sun, where the glaucous blue-green foliage and bright yellow flowers (often lasting through the winter) show to advantage. Given three or four years, it makes a nice little bush, needing little trimming to keep tidy. Planted in rosebeds, and between raspberry canes, it benefits flowers and fruit. But in the herb border, keep it away from basil and sage.

French Tarragon *Artemisia dracunculus*
Half-hardy perennial, to 2 ½ ft

The name *dracunculus* ('little dragon') may be derived from ancient times when this herb was used to treat snake-bites. In thirteenth-century Arabia, tarragon was taken with unpleasant medicines, to mask their taste. John Evelyn once wrote of tarragon: ' 'Tis high cordial and friendly to the head, heart and liver.' By Tudor times its popularity was well established in Britain, enhancing egg dishes and improving the often-strong flavour of chicken and red meats.

Use the leaves generously either with other herbs or as a distinctive flavour with fish or in salads; in pickles, herb butters and vinegar. Used with chervil, parsley and chives, tarragon is indispensable to *fines herbes*. It also gives the unique flavour to Sauces Bearnaise and Ravigote. Our forefathers quickly discovered tarragon needed to be used fresh; today, freezing enables it to be enjoyed all the year round. Although the French does lose much of its flavour in drying, the Russian tarragon (*A. dracunculoides*) is equally acceptable fresh, dried or frozen. Tarragon today is used commercially in perfumes and a range of liqueuers.

The leaves are rich in mineral salts and iodine, also Vitamins A and D. Infuse 1 oz of fresh leaves in 1 pint boiling water, and take to relieve flatulence and stimulate the appetite. Halitosis can temporarily be counteracted by chewing a few tarragon leaves. The coiling white roots used to be pounded to a pulp which was applied to aching teeth: a pleasant enough cure, and less dangerous than whisky!

If you are offered tarragon seed, it will be that of *A. dracunculoides,* the hardier, less popular, Russian sort. French tarragon's small, greeny-white flowers only rarely set seed in the British climate, so grow this herb from cuttings taken in autumn and over-wintered under glass. Divide mature plants every other year, since they soon deteriorate if left in a clump.

Whether under glass or outdoors, see that your plants get as much sun as possible, and fairly dry conditions. If you take the risk of over-wintering them outdoors, protect the crowns with a thatch of bracken or compost.

April

Herby Baked Potatoes
April

---

*The flowers appear on the earth; the time of the
singing of birds is come, and the voice of the
turtledove is heard in our land.*
(Song of Solomon 2:12)

April

STARTERS

Landcress Soup • Cheese Straws • Tuna on Toast

SAVOURY LIGHT LUNCHEON/
SUPPER DISHES

---

*Herby Baked Potatoes • Chicken Moussaka
• Artichokes and Bacon •*

DINNER (MAIN COURSE DISHES)

---

*Chicken aux Herbes • Sauerkraut au Köln
• Boeuf Stroganov •*

DESSERTS

---

*Pashka • Metropolitan Waffles • Peaches and
Cream*

BREAD AND CAKES

---

*Turkish Scones • Derbyshire Oatcakes
• Sprouted Loaf •*

HERBS OF THE MONTH

Garlic • Thyme • Spearmint • Lemon Balm

Except where otherwise stated, each recipe caters for four people

The year begins at different times for universities, diarists, gardeners and income tax boffins. For me, April (occasionally March), with the celebration of Easter, means the start of everything new, lengthening days and the promise in the garden of so much colour and fresh food ahead.

Victorian country vicarages invariably were endowed with large gardens. Mine runs to three acres, with woodland, and keeps the house in fruit and vegetables. For the best part of fifty years I've known the value of homegrown food, simply cooked, and varying according to the seasons. In the early days freezers were unknown so to enjoy, for example, soft fruit at Christmas, one needed to bottle it – and pray the seals were good. Many a time jars of raspberries or damsons would explode, staining even darker the black-oak Elizabethan cupboard in the dining-room.

With a couple of stone-benched pantries, I don't need a fridge, but the cavernous chest-freezer in the kitchen is never out of commission.

STARTERS

In our unheated tomato house, American landcress (Barbarea vulgaris) is burgeoning. It's a very worthwhile vegetable to grow, giving two seasons' yield from seed sown in April. Leaves can be picked as young as six weeks, and will continue to provide mineral-rich material for salads and soups for 15–17 months.

Landcress Soup

Serves 6
3 handfuls landcress or watercress
2 oz sunflower margarine
1 oz wholemeal flour
pinch of iodized sea salt
1 pint chicken and garlic stock
½ pint milk
½ pint cream

Chop the cress and blend into half the margarine. Melt the other half, add flour and salt. Heat gently. Gradually add stock, stirring to the boil. Gently add the cress and margarine mixture and re-heat, adding milk-slowly. Stir in the cream just prior to serving.

Iodized sea salt is recommended here in Derbyshire, an inland county, and goitre ('Derbyshire Neck') is a product of iodine deficiency – to be avoided if at all possible.

The disadvantage of having a lot of fingers in a lot of pies (inedible ones) means that sooner or later one is invited to join numerous committees – which seem to increase, no matter how practised one becomes at declining invitations. The advantage is that members either meet in my home, or converge for a meal before or after local meetings. A quick starter for such occasions is

Cheese Straws

2 oz butter
4 oz wholemeal flour
pinch of sea salt
pinch of orange mint, dried or chopped
3 oz crumbly white Cheshire cheese, grated
1 egg yolk
2–3 tsp cold milk

Rub fat into flour, salt and mint. Stir in the grated cheese and egg yolk, mixing with the milk. Cut into straws and bake on a baking sheet for 12–15 minutes at 400°F (200°C), Gas Mark 6.

Of an evening now I'll take Emma, the St Bernard, up the lane at the end of our Big Wood. Called the Priest Way, this lane had ecclesiastical connections centuries before either the church or this house was built. We go through the gate at the top, to the high fields where curlews have at last returned from their winter estuaries. Their autumn departure, like that of the swallows, often goes unnoticed; but how welcome is their return – the aerial gymnastics, glimpses of long, curved beaks, and – best of all – the penetrating cries that stop the cats in their tracks and bring a whiff of the sea to our so-inland county.

We return home with a forage-bag of greens – sweet cicely, chickweed, dandelions, milkmaids, hawthorn and field-cress: perfect for

Tuna on Toast

green salad
7 oz tuna flakes
4 rounds of wholemeal bread
parsley butter

Blend the salad with the tuna, to give a lovely colour-contrast. Toast the bread well on one side, lightly on the top, and spread generously with the parsley butter. Top with the tuna mixture. So simple!

LIGHT SAVOURY DISHES

At this time of the year geese from the southern estuaries fly over on their way to northern nesting grounds. Determined, disciplined honking is a lovely sound on a clear April afternoon, while I'm planting the new potatoes. There are still enough of last season's left to enjoy

Herby Baked Potatoes

Serves 6
6 large potatoes
6 rosemary stems, 6–8 in. long, with or without leaves
garlic clove, crushed
thyme butter (3 small sprigs to ¼ lb butter)

Wash and scrub potatoes (I grow the waxy, yellow-fleshed 'Red King Edward'). Pierce lengthways with a stainless steel skewer. Withdraw skewer and insert a rosemary stem in each potato. Prick all over with a fork. Rub with crushed garlic. Bake near the top of the oven at 400°F (200°C), Gas Mark 6, for 1 hour. Withdraw rosemary stems and cut each potato lengthways. Spread generously with thyme butter.

This is a conventional Moussaka, with chicken instead of lamb. I enjoyed it first in Moscow: perhaps, in 1973, chickens were more plentiful there than lambs! Still today, in many cold areas of Russia, the domestic hens are brought indoors for the winter, spending from October to March or April in the passage next to the kitchen. I think it's a wonderful idea, but have not yet copied it here.

Chicken Moussaka

4 medium or 2 large aubergines
salt and pepper to taste
1 garlic clove, chopped
6 tbsp olive oil
1 lb chicken meat, diced
3 tomatoes, chopped not skinned
1 bay leaf
½ pint chicken stock
1 oz sunflower margarine
1 oz wholemeal flour
½ pint soured cream
1 large egg, beaten

Peel and slice thinly the aubergines, arrange on a plate and salt liberally. Allow 30 minutes for extraction of the bitter juices, then drain, rinse in cold water, and dry on absorbent paper. In a deep pan, fry the garlic in a little oil. Add the chicken and fry until brown. Add chopped tomatoes, bay, seasoning and stock. Bring to the boil, cover and simmer for 30–40 minutes, when most of the liquid will have been absorbed. Using remainder of the oil, fry the aubergines until light brown, and drain again (or paint them with oil and grill them).

Butter a casserole dish. Arrange a layer of aubergine slices in the bottom, and cover with a layer of chicken. Carry on until all the ingredients are used, with aubergines as the topmost layer. In a saucepan, melt the margarine gently. Stir in the flour, and add soured cream, stirring all the time. Bring to the boil, season, and simmer for 2–3 minutes. Remove from heat and add beaten egg. Pour gently over the chicken and aubergine layers and cook at 350°F (180°C), Gas Mark 4, for 35-40 minutes. I like Moussaka with fresh wholemeal rolls and a green salad.

Jerusalem artichokes are so rewarding: from late September when I raid the row for Harvest Festival, until this month when the new shoots only add to the tubers' delicious flavour. This is a dish quickly prepared and even quicker eaten.

Artichokes and Bacon

Serves 6
6 thick rashers of lean bacon
olive oil
rosemary
2 lb Jerusalem artichokes
1 garlic clove, sliced
salt to taste
lettuce or endive to garnish

Fry the bacon in a little oil. Sprinkle the rashers with rosemary, and keep warm. Heat oil in the deep grill pan. Scrub and slice the artichokes. Add garlic and artichokes to the oil, and grill quickly until both sides of the slices are brown. Serve the artichokes and bacon with a garnish of lettuce or endive.

MAIN COURSE DISHES

I like my poultry poached: they taste so much better than when soused in fat, which either clings to the foil or spits around the oven. The charms of cooked goose have never smitten me; but from the time when we first ran poultry in the woods, I've loved chicken – whether Light Sussex, or the yellow-fleshed Rhode Island Reds, or the delicious pheasant-like Indian Game we bred when my father was alive.

Chicken aux Herbes

I stuff the bird's body-cavity with garlic – but then I grow an awful lot of garlic, and I firmly believe it is *the* most beneficial of herbs. You'll almost certainly not grow so much, and equally certainly you'll want to use fewer cloves for this recipe. But do use as many as you can. When cooked as thoroughly as my poached chickens are cooked, garlic not only fills the kitchen with an absolutely divine aroma guaranteed to clear sinusitis and catarrh – but the resulting taste is deliciously *mild*: believe me!

Rub the bird's flesh with dried or fresh sage, tarragon, thyme and parsley (or any combination, as they say in word games). Be generous with the sea salt. Use a large pan with a well-fitting lid. Cover the bird with water. Bring to the boil, then simmer gently, allowing 1 hour per pound. I like the flesh to fall off the bones and my guests appreciate boned meat.

The value of the stock-pot accumulates, for I leave the carcase in the pot, returning it to the boil at least once every 24 hours – which gives the most nutritious foundation for soups, stews and casseroles, and an aromatic kitchen into the bargain. Always have a stock-pot on the stove, and you've the next meal more than half-done.

This chicken can be served either hot or cold – with a green salad, in sandwiches, or even (flaked) as the backbone of a soup or stew. Truly, a multi-choice recipe (and my favourite into the bargain).

This recipe, with slight variations, is a very old one treasured by my friend in Cologne.

Sauerkraut au Köln

4 compact white cabbage hearts
¼ lb sea salt
¼ oz caraway seeds
butter and gravy

Remove the hard pith and shred cabbage finely. Mix in the salt and caraway, and press firmly into an earthenware pot. Press down and cover with a plate held down by a heavy weight. Keep in a warm place for 2 months, after which it's ready for use and needs then to be kept cool. Take out only as much as is required. Add to a knob of melted butter and gravy. Cook on a low heat until tender. Serve with pork or beef sausage.

I've never yet matched the Stroganov we enjoyed in Moscow and St Petersburg. Hope springs eternal, but the true Russian smetana *(sour cream) is unreproducible.*

Beef Stroganov

1 ½ lb stewing steak
1 clove garlic, halved
4 oz sliced flat mushrooms
2 oz butter
salt, pepper and thyme
water to top up cream
5 fl. oz soured cream
1 dessertsp wholemeal flour
2 tomatoes, sliced not chopped
1 dessertsp vinegar

Chop the meat into bite-sized pieces. In a deep pan fry garlic and mushrooms in butter until just brown, over gentle heat. Mix in the chopped meat, and season. Add water to the cream, to make ½ pint, and pour over the meat and mushrooms. Stir in flour, tomatoes and vinegar. Bring to the boil and simmer for 2 hours, covered. Serve with brown rice, broccoli spears and carrots, or a green salad.

DESSERTS

After the rigours of Lent, Easter comes as a time of refreshment in more ways than one. On Easter Eve I make Pashka, the traditional Russian Easter cheesecake – not a bit like our Western supermarket varieties. In Russia it's often made in a special mould, with the letters 'Х.В.' (ХРИСТОС ВОСКРЕСЬ – 'Christos Voskres' = 'Christ is Risen'). I make mine in a series of red bowls – precious, because they were the last present my father gave to my mother before he died in 1961.

Pashka

Serves 6–8
1 large egg
1 ½ lb soft curd cheese
2 ½ oz natural yoghurt
4 oz sultanas
2 oz nuts, chopped
2 oz sunflower margarine
1 tbsp clear honey
dash of vanilla or almond essence

Beat egg, and then mix with all the other ingredients together. Butter can be used instead of margarine, but is harder to mix. Leave the Pashka in its bowl until the next day, and then enjoy it. What could be simpler?

That's the Easter Pashka – the first of many I make in the year. Pashka is a meal in itself; it doesn't need any other additions. In Russia, particularly in the country areas, worshippers often take Pashka to the Easter service, after which families meet together for a meal in the churchyard. I always share the first Pashka of the season after church on Easter morning, when a group of us gathers round the TV to join in the celebrations from St Peter's in Rome. The high spot for me is when the Pope greets the Christians of Russia in their own tongue: 'Christos Voskres – Christ is Risen!'

On 14 May 1967, Liverpool's Metropolitan Cathedral of Christ the King was consecrated. We visited it the month before, when the great space under the lantern was just that. The contrast between this bravely modern building and the equally new but traditionally-styled Anglican Cathedral at the other end of Hope Street was dramatic.

We were in the city not only to visit the cathedrals, but to join friends from many parts of the country for a ninetieth birthday celebration in nearby Hesketh. There I was introduced to waffles, and immediately fell in love with them – at least, the Merseyside recipe. Although I've modified it over the years, we still call it after the cathedral which looked so lovely and so impressed us that day.

Metropolitan Waffles

6 oz plain flour
pinch of sea salt
3 tsp (level) baking powder
1 oz demerara sugar
2 eggs, separated
2 oz butter, melted
½ pint milk
dash of almond essence
pinch of lemon thyme

You'll need a waffle-iron for these. In a bowl mix flour, salt and baking powder lightly. Add sugar. Beat in egg yolks, and then add butter and milk, almond and thyme. Whisk the egg whites until stiff, and fold into the batter. Grease the waffle-iron and heat it. Brush it again with melted butter. Pour in some of the batter and brown quickly on each side. Eat hot, with maple syrup.

This is just a variation of an old theme. One day I'll give it a new name. It's a foretaste of summer, more than justifying freezers and the canning industry.

Peaches and Cream

4 bananas
8 peach halves (tinned or frozen)
blackberries, strawberries and plums, or any preserved fruit
raspberry ice cream
mint sprigs to decorate

Cut the bananas lengthways. Slice peaches thinly, and lay them down the centre of the banana slices. Add the mix of berries and sliced plums for colour. Top with ice cream decorated with mint. So simple, can we call it a recipe?

BREAD AND CAKES

April bees are busy working over the shimmering falls of alpine phlox and aubrieta on the terrace. One day – I've been promising for years – I'll keep bees, and tend hives, and collect honey. Until then, I'll buy honey at church fêtes, and from keepers who summer their hives on the moors. The latter produce a clear heather honey which makes delicious Turkish Scones – and much else!

Turkish Scones

2 oz butter
8 oz self-raising flour
2 oz clear honey
2 oz sultanas
generous pinch each of salt and mint
¼ pint milk

Rub butter into the flour as fine as possible. Stir in honey and sultanas. Add seasoning and mix with milk. Roll out dough and cut into generous triangles (roughly 3 ins per side and ⅓ – ½ in thick). Cook on buttered baking sheet at 425°F (220°C), Gas Mark 7, for 10 minutes. Serve as 'vicars', not 'curates' – i.e. split in half, and *both* buttered!

My cousin in Cornwall likes to take some home with her after a visit; my friend on the Shetland Isles – an Anglican Franciscan nun – begged me for the recipe when I introduced her to them on a snowy day here in February 1991. What are they? What else but Derbyshire Oatcakes! They're the best food made for toasting – but because of their size (nearly 10 in. across) and floppiness, use a grill pan with a rack, a griddle, or even a thick-bottomed frying pan instead of a toasting fork. Many are the variations; this is mine.

Derbyshire Oatcakes

½ lb plain flour
½ lb oatmeal
generous pinch of sea salt
1 tsp caster sugar
½ oz fresh yeast
½ pint warm water
lard

Add flour, oatmeal and salt to a warmed bowl. Cream the sugar and yeast and add to warm water. Mix all the ingredients together, stirring gently to an even batter. Cover and leave in a warm place for ½–1 hour to prove. Grease a griddle or pan with lard. Place over a gentle heat, and with a wooden ladle pour some batter on to the centre of the griddle or pan. Brown lightly on both sides.

It's usually better and more convenient to make a stock of oatcakes, putting aside enough for, say, a couple of days, and wrapping the rest individually in greaseproof or polythene (when cold) in the freezer. They keep well, and can be taken out and toasted from frozen.

I like mine newly toasted on the grill rack, cut into quarters and served on hot plates with lashings of butter; that's all – they're a meal in themselves. I've never seen a Derbyshire person eating the county's speciality with any other food.

Seed which is left over from sharing with our large and varied bird population now fills jars on the kitchen mantelpiece. Rinsed each day, growth is satisfyingly rapid. I like to use the sprouted seeds not only in salads, but in a variety of breads. It is nutritionally rich, and nowadays more and more seedsmen are offering an ever larger variety of sprouting seeds. Use when the sprouts are no more than ½ – ¾ in. long. CAVEAT: Don't just use any packs of birdseed; only that sold by health food shops and seedsmen, for growing.

Sprouted Loaf

There's a variety of seeds to choose from: alfalfa, fenugreek, alphotaco, mung . . . Decide which you like best and vary the quantities to taste. If you can't get sprouting seed, try variations on the basic wholemeal recipe with, say, 3 oz grated cheddar cheese or 4 oz sultanas.

chosen seeds (1 tbsp to 3 lbs flour)
2 eggs
1 oz parsnip, grated
a little parsley and chives, chopped

Chop the seeds fairly fine. Add the eggs, parsnip and herbs. Mix this into the wholemeal bread recipe (see January), and leave to prove as usual. Bake as for wholemeal bread.

Sometimes I add a sprouted mix to tea cakes, too. I'm forever mixing and matching. Here in Derbyshire we're fairly richly endowed with flour mills, which all make for variations in the wholemeal flour itself. In city centres you have probably just as many, if not more, brands of flour, so do experiment!

April is a good month: never too warm, often dry for most of the time, and ideal for catching up with all the estate work held in abeyance during the snows and storms of March. It's a month for the main sowings of new herbs, and transplanting earlier sowings.

HERBS OF THE MONTH

Garlic *Allium sativum*
Hardy perennial bulb, 12 in.

Enjoyed by the Israelites in Egypt; fed to the slaves who built the pyramids; revered in ancient China as protection against evil; prescribed for athletes competing at the earliest Olympic Games garlic has a long history of culinary and medicinal uses.

Like onions, but in greater proportions, garlic contains Vitamins A, B and C, and sulphur. *Always be generous with garlic in the kitchen:* the more you use, the greater success you'll have in keeping coughs and colds at bay. Give salad dressings zip with garlic vinegar: pound 8 garlic cloves, sprinkle with salt, cover with 1 pint boiling vinegar. Leave for a fortnight, strain off liquid, and bottle.

Garlic was used during World War I as a field-dressing, with strong antibacterial properties. At the onset of a cold, chew a raw garlic clove; never mind how your tongue tingles. In addition to fighting bronchial and catarrhal problems, garlic purifies the blood and helps fight arteriosclerosis and high blood pressure.

In the garden, garlic is anathema to peas and beans, but grow it among raspberries and blackcurrants for more fruit. Grown near peach trees it controls leaf-curl; and – surprisingly – in the rose garden enhances the scent of the flowers! If potato blight is a problem, spray with a freshly-made infusion of garlic.

Although hardy perennials, the bulbs should be divided and replanted each year.

The individual *cloves* are lifted in July and August, clustered together as a *bulb*, which is then dried and strung up in plaits as close to the kitchen as possible. Keep back a few cloves to plant in October, for next year's harvest. Given good rich soil, in full sun, they'll never disappoint you. Spring-planted cloves, in Britain, tend to make only a single bulb, instead of a cluster of cloves.

Thyme *Thymus vulgaris*
Hardy perennial, 6–8 in.

'I know a bank where the wild thyme blows,' said Oberon, in Shakespeare's *A Midsummer-Night's Dream* (II.i.249). Strictly speaking Oberon was referring to *Thymus serpyllum*, the thyme which makes those plush purple cushions, so effective in rock gardens. *T. vulgaris*, less cushiony, has more flavour and is the best sort for the kitchen.

Grown in the Hanging Gardens of Babylon, thyme was also the favourite strewing and antiseptic herb of the Greeks. Its attraction for bees was exploited in the valleys around Mount Hymettus (from which honey still makes its way to many countries of the world). In Egypt it was used extensively in embalming. By the sixteenth century Britain had thyme in all her herb gardens, and its antiseptic properties were put to good use in times of plague. When the London air left much to be desired, John Evelyn the diarist suggested thyme should be planted in gardens the length and breadth of the city.

Thyme can be used fresh, dried or frozen, and is best when cut prior to flowering. It is an essential ingredient of *bouquet garni:* use it when cooking rich or fatty meat. No amount of cooking spoils thyme's pungency, so use sparingly. I like it blended with cream cheese, and just a snippet in egg dishes. When gardening, a nibble of thyme staves off the pangs of hunger.

It's used today in toothpastes and mouthwashes. When drunk as a tea (1 oz dried thyme to 1 pint boiling water), it soothes sore throats, colds and bronchial ills. Thyme helps to promote white blood corpuscles and resist infection, and is beneficial for insomniacs.

When dried, hang a bunch of thyme in a wardrobe or airing cupboard, to deter moths and give a fresh scent. Thyme is excellent for herb sachets, cushions and *pot-pourris.*

Sow the seed in spring, and plant out either singly or in groups of three, along a sunny border edge. Thyme tolerates some lime in the soil, but not prolonged wet conditions. Over-winter some pots under glass. If left untrimmed, the little bushes go woody and die after a few seasons.

Spearmint *Mentha x spicata:* hybrid of *M. longifolia* and *M. suaveolens*
Hardy perennial, to 2 ft

In biblical times mint was regarded as valuable enough for the Pharisees to tithe it. Often it was strewn on synagogue floors; this practice was later copied in Italian churches, the mint becoming known as 'Erba Sancta Maria'. The Romans took mint with them on peaceable and not so peaceable travels, until it was known and appreciated throughout Europe. Further afield, the Japanese used it extensively in pomanders.

Nowadays, we value the culinary properties of mint rather than merely its scent, pleasant though that is. For mint vinegar: lightly pack fresh sprigs into a wide-necked, earthenware pot, fill with vinegar, strain after 2–3 weeks, and bottle in dark or opaque jars. Avoid using mint with garlic in cooking. Otherwise, it can be added – fresh or dried – to a variety of soups, chutneys, red and white meat, jellies, gravies and sauces.

Mint tea, taken hot or cold, is not only a refreshing drink, but a good reliever of indigestion. A strong infusion of hot mint tea is a safe and pleasant emmenagogue, and alleviates period pains.

Dried mint packed into sachets can be hung in cupboards, or strewn under the lining paper in drawers as an insect-repellent. Hang a bunch in the pantry, or lay a few sprigs on the food shelves, to discourage mice.

Take root-cuttings of mint every other year. Old plants are prone to rust disease which debilitates the host and spreads to neighbouring plants. Since there are at least 600 varieties of mint in cultivation today, a herb garden can be designed using only mints. The properties of mints vary considerably, making this a most fascinating and valuable herb family for kitchen, home, garden and medicine chest.

Lemon Balm *Melissa officinalis*
Hardy perennial, to 18 in.

This easily-grown herb has been valued in Mediterranean areas for more than 2,000 years. 'Balm' is a contraction of 'Balsam', and its lemony scent is most pungent when the leaves are used fresh. 'Melissa' comes from the Greek for 'honey-bee', and accounts for the common name 'Bee Balm'. It used to be grown around apples and other top fruits, to encourage pollinating bees – and today many apiarists rub balm on their hives when installing a new swarm.

The Swiss doctor, Paracelsus, in the seventeenth century, was generous in his praise and use of balm; his enthusiasm was echoed by John Evelyn, the diarist: 'Balm is sovereign for the brain, strengthening the memory, and powerfully chasing away melancholy.'

Balm adds a lemony fragrance to vinegars. Blend it with tarragon for an even more piquant flavour. Chop the leaves into salads, fish sauces and a variety of green vegetables just before serving. Line cake-tins with leaves before adding the mixture and cooking. Poultry can be sprinkled with fresh or dried leaves prior to cooking, or the herb can be incorporated in stuffings. The variegated form (*M.o.* var. *variegata*) is particularly pretty when used in fruit salads, custards and jellies; and lemon balm tea (hot or cold) is both a refreshing and soothing drink at any time of the day (use 1–1 ½ tsp herb to a cup of boiling water, and allow to stand for 8–10 minutes).

Rub on balm to alleviate the irritation caused by insect bites. Dry some of the leaves, and stitch handy sachets for use under pillows, in pockets and handbags, and among clothes in drawers and wardrobes. Use fresh balm in flower-arrangements, for long-lasting colour (in the case of the variegated form) and lemon scent.

There are two forms: the green-leaved, and the green-and-gold variegated. Grow the latter in partial shade, or the leaves will become scorched. In all but the most severe winters, many of the old leaves will stay fresh until the new ones begin to grow, making this herb virtually an evergreen.

May

Elderflowers.
May

He that tilleth his land shall be satisfied with bread.
(Proverbs 12:11)

May

STARTERS

---

*Ascension Treat • Soupe Archepiscopale
Broccoli Hors-d'oeuvre*

SAVOURY LIGHT LUNCHEON/
SUPPER DISHES

---

*Terrine de Lapin • Liver and Beans
• Russian Fish Salad •*

DINNER (MAIN COURSE DISHES)

Chelsea Pork Pie • Braised Guinea-fowl • Coulibiac

DESSERTS

---

*Rhubarb and Ginger Crumble • Anna's Delight
• Threeberry Pie •*

BREAD AND CAKES

---

*Derbyshire Barley Bread • Spring Lardy Cake
Hope Teacakes*

HERBS OF THE MONTH

Anise Hyssop • Chives • Sage • Lady's Mantle

Except where otherwise stated, each recipe caters for four people

---

As the forty days of Easter come to an end, and the sepulchre garden comes out of the church, I spend a lovely day gathering a thousand and more late daffodils for our Ascension Day Eucharist, when our wee church is host to congregations from churches in the town.

STARTERS

For 7 May, which was my mother's birthday, I decorate our 'vicarage' window in the church with daffodils, polyanthus, elm flowers, quince, rhododendrons, white cherry-blossom and creamy elderflowers. It would grieve me to deprive my elder trees (now too large to be called bushes) totally of their spring beauty, for then neither I nor the birds would have the joy of berries, come the autumn. However, I cut a few clusters here and there for our

Ascension Treat

12 elderflower clusters
½ pint double cream
2 tbsp tarragon vinegar
¼ tsp sugar
sea salt
4 peach halves (tinned or frozen)

Strip the flowers from their stems, and mix well into the cream. Add the vinegar (Russian tarragon is milder than the French) and whisk until fairly firm. Add a suggestion of sugar, and a pinch of salt. Serve the peaches individually in half-shells, and top generously with the cream. I like to serve immediately, with a few extra elderflowers sprinkled on top.

I've looked down on the shipping in our eastern sea lanes, from the Gulf of Finland to the English Channel, without any feelings of envy or nostalgia: but mal de mer *was no deterrent to sailing up (or was it down?) the river for luncheon at the Archbishop's Palace, York, some years ago. One doesn't visit the kitchens on such occasions, but by trial and not a few errors I've evolved a soup which I can now safely say is a lot closer than forty-second cousin to the superb dish we enjoyed in the palatial setting of the spiritual head of the Northern Provinces.*

Soupe Archepiscopale

2 parsnips, diced
2 carrots, diced
4 Jerusalem artichokes
½ teacupful Brussels sprouts, chopped
2 cloves garlic, chopped
1 oz butter
12 green beans, sliced
½ teacupful spinach, shredded
2 tomatoes, roughly chopped
1 ½ pints chicken stock
herbs in season
sea salt
chives or parsley to garnish

This is Derbyshire; further south you may need to settle for (tinned) carrots or beans instead of parsnips. Choose a large saucepan or enamelled casserole dish with a tight-fitting lid. Dice the root vegetables and garlic and sauté with the sprouts in the melted butter until they are slightly soft. Next add the green beans, spinach and tomatoes, and fry until the spinach goes limp. Add the stock, herbs (my favourites are tarragon, thyme and sage) and seasoning, bring to the boil and simmer for around 20 minutes. Sprinkle with fresh chives or parsley on serving.

The last of the broccoli has been shared with the pigeons, in the interest of pea and broad bean survival. Gardening needs to be of the give and take variety now and then – which sounds far more charitable than the shameful thought of a fat pigeon being an easier target for the moggies. These final little broccoli sprigs make a nice starter, which I use with shrimps and the last of the freezer's mushrooms. In Russia mushrooms are dried – in their millions; but, providing one wipes off any excess moisture, fresh mushrooms here freeze well.

What a mixture of conditions! While the Russian winter, though colder, is drier than our's, most of us have electric freezers instead of six-month snowdrifts. Yet the majority of houses in Russia are infinitely better heated than ours.

Broccoli Hors-d'oeuvre

8 oz broccoli spears
4 oz flat mushrooms, diced
1 ½ oz butter or sunflower margarine
1 tsp wholemeal flour
2 ½ fl. oz cream
2 ½ fl. oz chicken and garlic stock
sea salt
4 oz shrimps
chives to garnish

Cook the broccoli in water for 2–3 minutes. Fry the mushrooms quickly in butter until just browning. Add the broccoli and fry for 3–4 minutes. Mix in the flour, add the cream, stock and seasoning. Bring to the boil, and simmer for a further 2–3 minutes. Add the shrimps, and stir in gently. Serve in shells, and garnish with chives.

Some years ago, a friend visited with some seeds of sugar beet. Intrigued, I sowed a box and planted out the resultant hundred or so seedlings alongside the sweet pea row. At this altitude the roots don't bulk up much, but the leaves are very tasty cooked as spinach (with no salt), and are available all the year round. They taste delicious in smetana, *or sour cream.*

LIGHT SAVOURY DISHES

Usually the first cut of silage takes place around 20 May. While the grass lies wilting overnight the cats move in to see what food has been disturbed. Nature thus arranges a minimum of mouse, vole and rabbit remains in the morning's harvest. I don't begrudge the cats their voles and mice, but I'd be grateful if they'd leave a few more rabbits for one of my favourite dishes:

Terrine de Lapin

Marinade:
1 wine glass claret
6 bay leaves
12 juniper berries, crushed
2 cloves
2 tsp sea salt
Terrine:
2 rabbits
4 lb beef, minced
sea salt and pepper
1 ½ lb bacon rashers
1 tbsp each parsley, chives, coriander and oregano, finely chopped

Mix all the ingredients for the marinade. Remove meat from the rabbits and steep for 12 hours in the marinade.

Retain the offal – heart, kidneys and liver – and mince. Add to the minced beef. Season the mixture. Remove any rind on the bacon, and line four 1 pint terrine dishes with the rashers, keeping back some slices for covering.

Strain off the marinade. Lay the beef and offal mixture and herbs in layers on the bacon. Top with the rabbit meat, and pour on the marinade. Cover with the reserved bacon. Protect with foil, and put on the lid. Set in a bain marie in a pre-heated oven at 375°F (190°C), Gas Mark 5, for 1 ½ hours, removing the foil and lid for the final 10 minutes to allow the terrine to brown on top.

I like to serve this terrine hot for luncheons, cold for suppers – and it's a good stand-by for picnics. Pâtés need advance planning, so I make four at a time and keep a reserve in the freezer.

On a dry calm day, armed with crowbar and hammer, I set up the runner bean stakes, sawn on dormant winter days and stacked in the stable. I love runners – kidney beans, we used to

---

call them. Unless the frost whips in extra-early and blackens them in their prime, they're surely the most productive of vegetables. I like them all the year round, with liver as

Liver and Beans

1 lb runner beans
2 oz sunflower margarine
2 cloves garlic, chopped
1 tbsp coriander seeds
5 fl. oz soured cream
½ lb pig's liver, thinly sliced
sea salt

Mix the beans, margarine, garlic and coriander into the cream. Grease a pie dish, and pour in. Add the liver and season, cover with foil and bake at 350°F (180°C), Gas Mark 4, for 15–20 minutes. Serve with baked jacket potatoes.

In Russia we had fish every day: a rich variety of shapes, sizes and colours, the like of which Britain rarely sees, and inland Derbyshire never. Still, from those exotic meals in St Petersburg's grand dining-rooms stems my

Russian Fish Salad

½ lb halibut or cod, cooked and flaked
12 sardines
12 sild
½ lb shrimps, cooked
The salad:
½ lb salsify, boiled, skinned and cut into rounds
½ lb Jerusalem artichokes, boiled but not skinned, sliced
6 tomatoes, rosed
1 cucumber, sliced into matchsticks
¼ lb asparagus spears
3 hard-boiled eggs, chopped not sliced
lettuce, endive or radicchio
landcress
parsley
2 garlic cloves, puréed

Cook the halibut or cod by your preferred method. Flake the cooked flesh. Make up the salad on a large dish – I use an antique Chinese blue-and-white meat dish. Arrange the fish on top of the salad. I thicken any fish stock with double cream, and use as a salad-dressing (or in winter, as a fish soup starter).

Family and friends love this dish. I don't know why fish salads are not eaten more widely in Britain.

MAIN COURSE DISHES

When Sir William Pickford was appointed Master of the Rolls he took the title 'Lord Sterndale', after this village which he and his family loved so much as an out-of-London retreat. Of his two daughters, the younger – Mary – became one of the first women MPs; the elder, Dorothy, who divided her time between the Hall across the park here and Chelsea, was a very good friend. She died in 1971 and I still miss her.

We used to dine together in Chelsea week, for her London flat overlooked the Show grounds. One of her favourite recipes was enjoyed in Sloane Square, at the Hall here, and when she came across for a meal with me. It's been one of my stand-bys for many a dinner party.

Chelsea Pork Pie

I tried several pastries before deciding that rough puff suited best. A poll of family and friends decided likewise – out of predeliction, loyalty, truthfulness, or a combination of all three!

Rough puff:
8 oz wholemeal flour
¼ – ½ pint warm water
6½ oz butter
1 tsp garlic salt
Filling:
2 lb lean pork
1 tsp each of parsley, thyme, tarragon, coriander, anise hyssop, and Lady's mantle
1 clove garlic, chopped
sea salt
1 small egg

Mix the flour and water and roll out. Cut butter into little wedges and spread on mix, and salt. Roll up. Roll out 4 times, sealing in a polythene bag for 20 minutes before each rolling session. Add a 10 minute resting period before finally shaping the pastry.

Dice the meat into fairly large chunks, and blend in the herbs, including garlic. Season. Fill the pastry to within ¾ in. of the top. Let your artistry run riot with the pastry lid: mine is different with each pie. Beat the egg, and brush liberally over the top. Cook at 375°F (190°C), Gas Mark 5, for an hour. Reduce to 350°F (180°C), Gas Mark 4, and cook for a further 30 minutes. I like to eat this pie hot – every time.

During the war we kept a couple of pigs each year. Large Whites, they were, and jolly good to eat. From my earliest days, the time of November and December was associated with the finger-blistering work of salting great portions of pork, on the stone benches in our cellars; of the old copper being brought into annual service and the rich scents of boiling meat; of my mother's deliciously steaming dishes of 'scraps' – the offcuts so tasty to nibble in between salting; the great suppers for family and friends who gathered, however early, to celebrate another Christmas . . .

There are so many happy memories of those otherwise-fraught days, when Mr Hitler's ironmongery fell too close for comfort, and his Luftwaffe aimed for the bomb-store near Buxton, and the stately homes of Haddon and Chatsworth barely a dozen miles away to the south-east.

My large ginger and white puss Mishka may have a good Russian name, but he has Hitler-like tendencies as far as pigeons are concerned. We are overendowed with wood pigeons in May, certainly; but Mishka invariably times his culling of weakly poults to coincide with my showing friends round the garden. Why, I wonder, does the value of a catch increase in proportion to the covetous attention of other moggies? As we traverse path after feathered path my guests could be forgiven for thinking Mishka had wiped out the pigeon population of Derbyshire.

My father liked pigeon pie, but I prefer guinea-fowl – and the feathers when cured are blissfully soft in pillows and cushions.

Braised Guinea-Fowl

One fowl will be sufficient for 2–3 servings
1 guinea-fowl
tarragon
wholemeal flour to coat
butter
6 rashers streaky bacon
1 wine glass claret

Rub the flesh with tarragon, and leave a little bunch in the body cavity. Coat the birds with wholemeal flour and brown in hot fat. Remove and place in a casserole dish, lined with streaky bacon. Add more tarragon to taste, mix claret with the fat and pour into the casserole. Cover and cook at 325°F (170°C), Gas Mark 3, for an hour or until the meat is tender.

I always serve guinea-fowl with Duchesse potatoes, whole carrots and sugar snap peas.

The young rooks of early hatchings are learning to fly. It's a good season this time, with few of the mortalities that an early-May drought often brings. Occasionally the cats will stalk a half-feathered youngster, but its strong beak and raucous cries – not to mention the basso-profundo warnings from Ma and Pa aloft – usually prompt the moggies to opt for discretion.

In the thirties, the colonel of the village would organize an annual shoot. Now our rooks are unmolested, save for the occasional pot-shotter whose interest is as short-lived as his shots are wild. Colonel Sowler was a grand man: an old Harrovian, he lived to be 93. Our friend Doreen Sowler was a frequent guest here, and was one of the few who remembered with relish the generous hospitality of the Grimshawes of Errwood Hall. The last of that family passed on when, in the late thirties, Errwood received its quietus and Stockport Corporation flooded the Goyt Valley to provide yet another reservoir for urban consumption. Today one can visit the sad ruins of the once-stately home of a reclusive but hospitable family. The Grimshawes were Roman Catholics – the small shrine and graveyard are above the water-level, as are scores of beautiful rhododendrons originally imported from China at the turn of the century, as ballast on their yacht.

They were also endowed with an accomplished chef, who treated his guests to exotic recipes. From Miss Sowler's vivid descriptions I amended a lobster concoction into something less extravagant, but now a firm favourite with us. Not surprisingly, it's ended up very similar to a dish the Russians know as

Coulibiac

5–6 servings
8 oz brown rice
1 lb mushrooms
2 cloves garlic, chopped
2 oz butter
pinch of sea salt
pinch of marjoram
2 lb cod
1 pint soured cream
3 hard-boiled eggs
3 thin Derbyshire oatcakes, or pitta bread
1 lb puff pastry (prepared)
1 egg for glazing
soured cream and chopped chives to garnish

Boil the rice for 30 minutes. Drain, and set on one side. Slice the mushrooms (I like the big 'flats', which have so *much* more flavour than buttons). Fry the garlic in a little of the butter until brown. Add the mushrooms, salt and marjoram, and cook for 5 minutes. Stir in the rice, and allow to cool.

Cook the fish gently for 15 minutes in half the soured cream. Allow to cool. Drain, and flake the fish, removing any bones. Slice hard-boiled eggs. Re-heat the mushroom mixture, and warm the oatcakes.

Roll out the pastry (see December) into a rectangle (around 9 × 15 in.). Trim the sides and keep the bits to decorate the top. Brush with beaten egg and lay 1½ oatcakes (trimmed to size) on the pastry. On these add a layer of the mushroom mixture, followed by a layer of fish and the eggs. Continue adding layers of mushroom and fish, and top with the rest of the oatcakes, allowing them to overlap. Seal the edges.

Pierce a hole in the top for ventilation, decorate with the pastry left-overs, and glaze with beaten egg. Cook on a flat tray at 425°F (220°C), Gas Mark 7, for 30–35 minutes, until the top is brown. Serve hot in slices, with a garnish of soured cream and chopped chives.

DESSERTS

My mother was born in Yorkshire and, although she spent most of her life in Derbyshire, loved to visit her home county whenever possible. In the sixties and early seventies I remember motoring very often past acres of rhubarb fields, for which Yorkshire was justly famous. Now, alas, much of that crop has given way to industrial sites and/or motorways.

We grow a lot of rhubarb here because we like it a lot. May sees the first two major rhubarb-freezing sessions of the year. I cut the stems into 1 in. pieces and freeze them raw in 2 lb bags, allowing 1 dessertsp demerara sugar to each bag.

One of our most-served desserts is

Rhubarb and Ginger Crumble

2 lb rhubarb
6 oz demerara sugar
1 tbsp ginger mint, finely chopped
2 tbsp water
3 oz sunflower margarine
6 oz wholemeal flour
¼ pint double cream
1 tbsp clear honey
3 tbsp ground ginger

Chop the rhubarb into 1 in. pieces and three-quarters fill a baking dish. Dust over with half the sugar, and a little of the mint. Add cold water. Rub together the margarine and flour until crumbly. Add the rest of the sugar and mint, and press on to the fruit. Cook at 375°F (190°C), Gas Mark 5, for 45 minutes. Serve hot, with a topping of whipped cream, honey and ginger.

My mother's cooking was taken to families in trouble of one sort or another in the forties and fifties – often the trouble was bereavement, news of which always comes fast to a vicarage. I well remember in winter carrying baskets of delicious smelling, still-warm baked goods through the parish. Sometimes we'd stay talking for so long night would fall, and the journey back through the woods and along the lane, if we'd forgotten torches, was quite an adventure.

In the summer we'd take baskets of strawberries. New visitors to the garden have over the years marvelled at how we could eat so much fruit – for at one time the strawberry beds accounted for a good third of the large kitchen garden. A lot of them – either frozen or fresh – have been enjoyed in

Anna's Delight

named after a chum of many years ago.

1 ½ lb fresh strawberries
8 sponge fingers
3 egg whites
6 oz caster sugar
juice of half an orange
2 tbsp claret
¼ pint dry white wine
½ pint double cream

Into a glass bowl put half the fruit. Add 4 sponge fingers, then remainder of fruit (keeping back a few for decoration), and the other 4 sponge fingers. Whisk egg whites into half the sugar, and gently fold in the remaining sugar. Blend in the orange juice, claret and white wine. Whisk the cream, and fold in. Pour or spoon carefully over the fruit mixture and leave in a cool place for 2–3 hours. Decorate with strawberries just before serving.

The famous Bakewell Pudding came about as a result of a catastrophe; many have been the variations since produced. I remember one catastrophe here which also had a happy ending – and one which lived up to its name. It's not good culinary policy to try to do two, or three, jobs at the same time; nor is it invariably the case when you turn a knob to 'off' that the cooker will respond. The day was the Feast of Ascension: I was boiling a chicken, and the dog needed to be taken for a walk before our Eucharist service. We returned from the park to find the kitchen foggy with steam, the pan without a bottom, and the chicken giving a whole new meaning to the title 'pot-roast'. Those were the days when we cooked in aluminium pans . . .

Another catastrophe, which resulted in a 'new' dish becoming an old favourite, came some years later. I plonked the last of the season's blackcurrants into a pan without adding any water. Faced with barely half a pan of useable fruit and guests about to arrive, I raided the freezer . . . The result was so simple, it was hardly a recipe – but the guests loved it, and still do.

Threeberry Pie

6 oz strawberries
6 oz raspberries
6 oz gooseberries
7 oz puff pastry (prepared)
2 egg whites
2 oz sugar (you may like a little more)

Heat all the fruit together until nearly boiling. Strain off the juices, and add the fruit to prepared pastry (see December) in a pie dish. Whip the egg whites until stiff, and blend in the sugar. Spread over the fruit and bake at 300°F (150°C), Gas Mark 2, until the meringue is crisp.

In extremis, crumbled biscuits with a binding of syrup or honey can be used in place of the pastry – but it's good policy always to have a reserve stock of pastries in the freezer.

BREAD AND CAKES

Now the rows of barley and wheat need to be strung against wind damage. Soon the cats will escape from the afternoon sun to lie along the shady, pleasantly-rustling avenues of corn. Without the strings (nowadays, sadly, the old 'hay-band' has given way to plastic baler twine) the tall stems would quickly be flattened by natural or feline causes.

Derbyshire is well-endowed with corn mills. Those of us who can't grow sufficient cereals to warrant milling can buy freshly-ground flour at the mill. Most of my corn decorates our church, and nearby ones, in sheaves at Harvest Festivals. In days of yore, when our family was larger, we kept bins of different flours in 'Dale House', a quaint little building on the east side of the courtyard. Flour bins (or spanking new shiny dustbins, if you have less space) are wonderfully mouseproof.

I use barley flour to make delicious

Derbyshire Barley Bread

The gluten content in barley is fairly low, so bread made wholly with barley flour tends not to rise and falls apart when cut. So I mix flours.

1 ½ lb barley flour
1 ½ lb wholewheat flour
1 tbsp garlic salt
pinch of tarragon
3 ½ oz butter
2 oz fresh yeast
warm water

Sift the flour into a bowl, and add the salt and tarragon. Rub in the butter. Cream the yeast in a little of the water, stir in to mixture and add sufficient water to knead to a moist dough. Leave to prove in a warm place overnight (a practice I've copied from 'North o' the Border'). Set oven to 425°F (220°C), Gas Mark 7. Re-knead, and bake in 1 lb tins. Allow 15 minutes at full heat; turn the tins by 90 degrees, and reduce to 375°F (190°C), Gas Mark 5, for 20 minutes. Test by knocking the bottom of the loaves: if they sound hollow, they're done.

Ascension Day and May see the first of the Derbyshire Well Dressings, when villages decorate their wells and springs with floral pictures, often of a biblical nature. Onto the wooden frame is pounded damp clay, into which the flower petals, twigs, foliage, rice grains, inter alia, *are pressed. The effect is stunning and draws visitors from all over the country, and beyond.*

One of the first, and always at Ascensiontide, is Tissington village, about 10 miles from here and with five wells. The service of blessing takes place on Ascension morning, and thereafter the wells stay decorated until the following Monday. From now until early autumn, each weekend will see at least two or three well dressings in our county.

One of the delightful spin-offs from well dressings is an influx of visitors whom one may see only infrequently. Because they may drop in quite unannounced, I bake a lot of Spring Lardy Cake this month: it's a well-proven favourite.

My recipe is so unlike the conventional lardy cake – a bit on the rich side for regular consumption, but fine for those occasions when you need to serve virtually a meal in a helping.

Spring Lardy Cake

1 lb wholemeal dough, risen but uncooked
4 oz butter
4 oz demerara sugar
4 oz sultanas
4 tsp sesame seeds
½ tsp mixed spice
olive oil
milk

Have ready a 8 × 10 in. roasting tin. Roll out the dough, to around ¼ in. thick. Flake a third of the butter onto it, together with a third of the sugar, fruit, seeds and spice. Roll up the dough, and repeat this procedure a second and third time – with the lightest of light touches.

Grease the tin, roll out and press the dough into it. Cover with a cloth and leave in a warm place to prove (for at least 2 hours). Brush the top with milk and sprinkle it with more sesame seeds. Bake at 425°F (220°C), Gas Mark 7, for 30 minutes. Eat hot or, if you can wait long enough, in cold buttered slices.

'Live in Hope, die in Castleton' they used to say in the valley not far from here, which has a string of villages west to east: Edale, Castleton, Hope, Bamford and Hathersage. My mother lived in Hope, and went to a school in Hathersage. Her old school house still stands. It was in those early days at Hope, before the first war, that Mother learned how to make these super teacakes, by watching (mostly) and helping (a little) my grandmother's French cook. Perhaps, in deference to Pierre, they should be called Teacakes à l'Espérance.

To be baked with hope and eaten with pleasure.

Hope Teacakes

3 lb wholemeal flour
3 oz sugar
3 tsp salt
3 tsp basil
pinch of caraway seed
3 oz butter
2 oz fresh yeast
1 ½ pints warm milk
6 oz sultanas

Mix the dry ingredients as you would for bread. Tear, don't chop, the delicate basil leaves. Rub in the butter. Cream the yeast with a little of the milk, and add with the rest of the milk to the dry ingredients. Mix, adding the sultanas. Knead well – I knead in the bowl, but you may prefer a floured board. Cover with a cloth and leave to rise in a warm place for 2 hours at least.

Grease some baking trays. Re-knead the dough, and divide into 15 cakes. Set these on the trays, brush with milk and decorate with caraway seed. Allow to prove in a warm place for another hour. Cook at 400°F (200°C), Gas Mark 6, for 15–20 minutes. Slice in half, and serve immediately with plenty of butter.

HERBS OF THE MONTH

Anise Hyssop *Agastache foeniculum*
Hardy perennial, to 2 ft

This herb is prized in America as a bee plant, since it carries its colourful spires of bright purple flowers for several months. Mexican in origin, logically it shouldn't be winter-hardy in Britain. The name is derived from the Greek *aga* (much) and *stachys* (a spike), referring to the eye-catching flower spikes produced for much of the summer.

The dried leaves make an interesting seasoning for meat and poultry dishes. They have an aniseed-taste which, combined with the colour of the flowers (though not their shape), accounts for the common name of this herb which is slowly becoming better known in Europe. Use the fresh leaves, and the flowers, in both vegetable and fruit salads. The fresh or dried leaves torn or sprinkled on courgettes and fried in sunflower oil, make a delicious entree to a meal where the main course consists of pork or rich poultry, like goose or duck. I also use anise hyssop with Jerusalem artichokes, Swiss chard and asparagus peas, as well as in Ratatouille. Shred fresh leaves into cakes, scones and pastries; jams and jellies; ice cream and custards. Children love the flavour; freeze some leaves in ice cubes for the winter, and add to sauces.

Infused as a tea, it's good for the digestion, and can act as a mild sedative when taken on going to bed. Chew a leaf or two to freshen the breath, after garlic or curried meals. A sachet or two of dried anise hyssop in the car is said to ward off travel sickness.

Hang a bunch of fresh leaves in the kitchen to deter flies. The flowers are long-lasting in flower-arrangements, and attractive as brown spires when dried.

Bees searching for late food well into the autumn appreciate a few flowers left on the plants until the frosts. Anise hyssop likes full sun, and a good rich soil. Propagate by seed or root division in the spring. The young leaves have a pretty purply tinge. Grow it hither and yon in the vegetable patch, to encourage good pollination of other crops such as peas, beans and strawberries.

Chives *Allium schoenoprasum*
Hardy perennial, to 1 ft

Four thousand years ago the Chinese in their wisdom prized chives and, like good hosts, pressed some upon Marco Polo when he visited their country. The wide dissemination of chives in the West is partly due to the explorer's unequivocal appreciation of this pretty herb.

But Culpeper was not too smitten with its charms, declaring: 'I confess I had not added these, had it not been for a country gentleman, who by a letter certified to me that amongst other herbs I had left these out. They are indeed a kind of leeks, hot and dry in the fourth degree.' John Louden, the Victorian writer-cum-gardener, is much kinder: 'No cottage garden ought to be without chives' – though the reason he gives is for mixing chives into the food for young chickens, ducks and turkeys!

All parts of the plant are edible: the globular mauve flowers colour up a salad; the leaves, like those of any monocotyledonous plant, can be cut freely with no detrimental effects on the bulb; and the bulbs themselves, if you can spare them, can be shredded raw or cooked like onions. Chop a few leaves over the vegetables just before serving, as prolonged cooking wastes the delicate flavour of chives. Use raw as a garnish for egg and cheese dishes, salads and soups.

Chives stimulates the appetite, and if used as a regular part of the diet, helps combat anaemia.

Chives planted around fruit trees will deter scab; in rosebeds they keep black-fly at bay; and among carrots they repel the pestilential carrot-fly. Plant the bulbs 6 in. or so apart, in good, free-draining soil, in a sunny position; or grow from seed in late spring and plant out in small clumps for the first season. Lift and divide the mature clumps every three or four years.

Sage *Salvia officinalis*
Evergreen shrub, to 2 ½ ft

The name comes from the Latin *salvere*, 'to save': sage promotes good health. Dedicated to Zeus and Juniper in ancient times, sage was revered as a cure for sterility. From the sixteenth century in Britain, sage butter became popular as a fasting dish in the Church. It was also mixed with honey as a remedy for consumption. Sage tea used to be prized so highly in China, that 'China' tea was traded for sage from Dutch merchants. Culpeper said of sage that it is profitable for 'lowness of spirits'. Doubtless he was familiar with the ubiquitous 'Sage Ale', which lifted more than spirits.

Shredded sage leaves add a pungent taste to stuffing for rich meat and poultry. My county's delicacy, Derby Sage Cheese, is deservedly well-known, but try adding this herb to soft cheese, too. Place whole leaves on grilled or roasting meat; and lamb's liver cooked in sage leaves is a dish to be remembered. Whole leaves can be lightly brushed with olive oil and grilled with courgettes to accompany roast duck. Sage and apple jelly is a delicious preserve; try a little sage, too, with rosehip syrup, where it reduces some of the sweetness. The pretty purple flowers are decorative scattered in salads.

Sage tea is good for indigestion, colds, nervous tension and depression. The dried leaves yield an antibiotic oil after distillation. Burn leaves in a room as a disinfectant, and to annul cooking smells. Infuse fresh or dried leaves – add a dash of lemon and honey – and use as a gargle and mouthwash, and as a drink to ease laryngitis, tonsillitis and sore throats. It's also beneficial to the liver, stimulates menstrual flow and reduces unwanted milk in nursing mothers – but in this latter case, take only for two or three days, as prolonged use can produce toxic reactions. Rheumatic sufferers can obtain relief from using an ointment made from 2 tbsp shredded leaves to ½ lb melted lard.

Dried sage leaves sewn into sachets and slipped between clothes in airing cupboards and drawers, act as an insect-repellent.

Give sage plants full sun and well-drained soil. Prune fairly hard to keep the bushes tidy, but never cut back into the old wood which will not produce new shoots. Take cuttings in summer, since sage deteriorates after four or five years, when the tired bushes need to be replaced. Bees love sage, but rue and sweet basil don't, so keep the sage well away from these herbs. Even in Roman times, it was recognized that iron implements and sage didn't agree: today science has proved that iron salts are indeed anathema to sage.

Lady's Mantle *Alchemilla vulgaris*
Hardy perennial, to 1 ft

In mediaeval times the silvery drops of moisture which collect in the folds of Lady's mantle leaves each night were deemed to have magical powers, and were carefully collected and prized by alchemists (so, *Alchemilla*). From the same period also, perhaps in an ecclesiastical attempt to refute magic, stemmed the plant's dedication to Our Lady. It was valued as a treatment for so many gynaecological ills, it soon became known as 'a lady's best friend'. In later times, a German herbalist claimed that regular use of alchemilla could reduce by one-third all gynaecological operations.

The young leaves can be shredded or torn into salads, where they give a tangy, bitter taste. I like them blended with radicchio (a type of chicory).

An infusion of the leaves stimulates the appetite, but is primarily used for treating heavy menstrual flow and diarrhoea. In veterinary medicine, *alchemilla* preparations are used to treat diarrhoea in animals. A decoction of the root (fresh or dried) staunches bleeding from open wounds and acts as an antiseptic. For skin problems use the juice of leaves and stems, extracted by a blender. Allow to dry before rinsing off with warm water. Used regularly, it lightens freckles. A tepid wash of *alchemilla* is used in Switzerland to relieve tired eyes.

Lady's mantle is a good plant for hanging-baskets. The flowers can also be dried for sachets, *pot-pourris* and winter arrangements. When boiled, the leaves yield a green dye for wool.

Give this pretty little herb moist soil and partial shade. Sow seeds in spring, divide plants in autumn. A larger plant, *A. mollis*, with similar properties to *A. vulgaris*, is a favourite with flower-arrangers.

When you go on holiday to the mountains, keep an eye out for the tiny Alpine Lady's Mantle – our herb in miniature, still with each delicate leaf preserving the distinctive shape of the old-fashioned lady's mantilla, and still clasping in its folds each morning that intriguing little silvery drop.

June

Poppies in variety
June

——————————————————

I am the rose of Sharon, and the lily of the valleys.
(Song of Solomon 2:1)

——————————————————

June

STARTERS

Tomato and Basil Soup • St Peter Salad
• Asparagus Dip •

SAVOURY LIGHT LUNCHEON/ SUPPER DISHES

Paella Alexanders • Fish, Sandwich Style
• Liver and Fennel Pâté •

DINNER (MAIN COURSE DISHES)

Turkey Marengo • Summer Goulash
• Oregano con Vivo •

DESSERTS

Strawberry Dip • Fruit Picnic • June Syllabub

BREAD AND CAKES

Rye Bread • Fruit Buns • Strawberry Torte

HERBS OF THE MONTH

Sweet Basil • Alexanders • Oregano • Fennel

Except where otherwise stated, each recipe caters for four people

---

June is a beautiful month, seeing the end of the frosts, gloriously long days, and colour – colour everywhere. But roses? My mother was a rosarian, but I love only the great spreading Rosa moyesii *'Geranium', which scatters its scarlet petals hither and yon after a mere three or four days, but gives me hips for masses of syrup, come autumn; and* R. damascena, *whose light- and dark-pink slashed multi-petalled clusters peek in at the study window for most of the summer.*

So in this garden June is the month of poppies: the yellow Welsh poppies (just a few orange), which grow everywhere, and delight until the frosts; extravagant Oriental 'Allegro' poppies, flaunting great crinkly cups of black-spotted orange and red, which look as though they need ironing; delicate pale-orange wild poppies, allowed to poke up in any place they choose; and the crème de la crème, *violet-blue Tibetan poppies – how I love them, and how often I try to grow more from seed! Fortunately they reproduce vegetatively, with extreme goodwill.*

June is also the prime month of unexpected guests, making the most of an all-too-brief lull before their own fruit harvesting claims hours of dedication.

STARTERS

For many years I believed basil had too delicate a constitution for this Peakland garden. Then a friend gave me some seed and, well, who wastes an opportunity like that? And who, after the experience of cooking with fresh basil, will ever stop growing it?

Tomato and Basil Soup

Serves 6
1 lb ripe tomatoes
1 oz butter
1 clove garlic, chopped
sea salt to taste
3 oz brown rice
2 pints chicken stock
2 oz fresh basil, torn not chopped

Skin the tomatoes (but save the skin to shred into butter for a new-bread spread: tomato skins are far too nutritious to waste), leaving the seeds in, and quarter. In a deep pan, melt butter and fry garlic until nearly brown. Add tomato and seasoning, then gradually blend in rice and stock, with basil. *Never* chop basil – it's too frail – tear the leaves instead. Bring to boil, cover, and simmer for 20–25 minutes.

Sometimes I add a few mushrooms – but it's better to wait until the more flavourful wild ones are in season.

Salad days are here with a vengeance. The choice of fresh leaves and shoots is greater than at any other time. St Peter's Day falls on 29th June but we enjoy this salad on many other occasions, too.

St Peter Salad

Serves 6–8
3 butterhead lettuces
8 leaves Batavian endive
leaf mixture: rocket, coriander, French sorrel, oregano, alexanders, dill, chives and landcress
olive oil
little stem ginger
1 clove garlic
croûtons
parsley to garnish

Wash and drain the leaves. Use unblanched endive, for a tang to offset the bland lettuce flavour. Toss in oil. Chop garlic and ginger (this is a super combination, much used in Chinese cookery), and add to the salad, tossing again. Fry croûtons and use to decorate with parsley.

The last job my father and I did together in the garden was to weed the asparagus bed. That day was 8 June 1961, the day a young Catherine Worsley was the Duke of Kent's white-rose bride, in York Minster. Ever since, asparagus has always had a special place in my menus.

Asparagus Dip

Serves 6
18 spears asparagus
2 tbsp fennel leaves
¾ lb soft curd cheese

Cook and drain asparagus. Blend fennel into cheese – so simple! If you prefer, blend in asparagus as well, and serve as a spread on hot, parsley-buttered toast.

LIGHT SAVOURY DISHES

Some years I don't manage to get to the annual meeting of the S. Th. Diploma holders at Lambeth Palace, with its service in the chapel at which new diplomas are conferred. Tea follows afterwards in the spacious drawing-room at the end of that vast corridor lined with imposing portraits of former archbishops . . . and the equally imposing collection of magnolias in the quadrangle. But memories of Lambeth days linger . . . I always take Paella Alexanders in the boot of the car to eat cold on the journey home.

Paella Alexanders

Serves 6
6 chicken breasts
1 garlic clove, chopped
olive oil
1 lb Basmati rice
1 pint apple juice
1 pint chicken stock
½ tsp turmeric
½ tsp each coriander, oregano and burnet
sea salt
3–4 sausages
¼ lb alexanders roots, grated
2 oz broad beans
2 oz peas
8 oz shrimps, cooked
8 oz prawns, cooked

Fry chicken and garlic in oil until brown. Cover, and allow to simmer until cooked. Cook rice in apple juice and stock with turmeric, herbs and seasoning. Cook sausages quickly under the grill and at the same time cook the alexanders, broad beans and peas. Arrange a bed of rice on a serving dish, and decorate as the fancy takes you using all the ingredients – it'll turn out different every time. Delicious, hot or cold.

These club sandwiches were our mainstay the Saturday we drove nearly 700 miles to Edinburgh and back: taking in Durham, Abbotsford, Jedburgh and Dumfries.

Fish, Sandwich Style

wholemeal malted bread
salmon with fennel
cod with parsley
prawns with oregano

For picnics or long car drives, TV suppers or garden party cake-stalls, make triple-decker sandwiches with this mix – and be thankful for tinned fish (once in a while)!

Parsonage-houses – whether 'old' or not – are still inseparably linked with coffee mornings and the like. Fortunately, the Victorian house can cope, space-wise, even when the rain comes down. It helps if the hostess has thought to make a good stock of pâté in advance.

Liver and Fennel Pâté

Serves 14–16
1 garlic clove, whole
1 bay leaf
1 pint milk
2 lb pigs liver
1 lb lean bacon rashers
12 anchovy fillets
salt and pepper to taste
4 oz fennel leaves
½ tsp nutmeg
2 oz butter
2 oz wholemeal flour
2 eggs

Boil garlic and bay in milk. Allow to stand for 20 minutes. Mince liver, 12 oz bacon and anchovy finely, and season with salt and pepper, nutmeg and fennel. Melt butter, add flour and heat gently for 2 minutes. Stir in milk. Bring to boil and cook for a further two minutes. Blend in meat mixture. Add beaten eggs. With remaining bacon, line 2 lb loaf tins, allowing rashers to hang over the edges. Add pâté mix, and fold rashers over the top. Cook sealed in foil for 2 hours at 325°F (170°C), Gas Mark 3. Freezes well.

MAIN COURSE DISHES

In the churchyard at Kirk Hallam, not too far from here, is a stone to Samuel Cleator, who died in 1811. His epitaph runs:

True to his King, his Country was his glory,
When Bony won, he said it was a story.

Associations can be long-lived: I always think of Samuel Cleator when making this next dish. He must have been quite a character.

Turkey Marengo

Serves 6
1 clove garlic, whole
2 oz butter
6 lb turkey slices
3 tbsp olive oil
1 oz wholemeal flour
½ pint white wine
¼ pint chicken stock
6 tomatoes, sliced
1 lb mushrooms, sliced
½ cucumber, sliced
1 tsp each fennel, rocket and bergamot
½ tsp thyme
sea salt
dash of brandy

Fry garlic and turkey in butter and oil until brown. Dust with flour and stir until fat is taken up. Add wine and stock, and bring to the boil. Allow to simmer while slicing tomatoes, mushroom and cucumber. Add all three to pan and season with herbs and salt. Cover, and simmer for 1 hour, stirring occasionally to prevent sticking. Add brandy a few minutes before serving. I like Marengo with unbuttered baked potatoes.

I've a soft spot for Goulash – perhaps because it allows for so many variations, and also because I quickly found in my early cooking days, one can't go wrong with it! I'm sure mine is not a distant cousin to the original Bogrács Gulyás – but never mind.

Summer Goulash

1 clove garlic, sliced
1 ½ oz sunflower margarine
1 ½ lb good stewing steak, diced
½ tsp caraway seeds
¼ tsp each French sorrel, thyme and chives
4 oz alexanders root or carrot, grated
1 ½ tbsp paprika
salt to taste
1 ¾ pints beef stock
6 tomatoes, quartered
2 lb potatoes, diced

In a large casserole, fry garlic gently in margarine. Increase the heat. Add diced meat, chopped herbs, grated alexanders or carrot and seasoning. Fry for 5 minutes, stirring so that the meat browns on all sides. Reduce heat, add ½ pint stock and simmer in open pan for 1 ½ hours, adding more stock if the mixture begins to dry out. Add quartered tomatoes, diced potatoes and remainder of stock. Bring to boil and simmer for 15 minutes.

This is a much more colourful version of the conventional chilli con carne. I first ate it at a convent, after attending a Service of Profession. Since then it's been modified according to taste and my garden's June beneficence.

Oregano con Vivo

Serves 6
4 oz peas
4 oz broad beans
2 cloves garlic, chopped
little olive oil
1 lb liver, diced
8 oz tomatoes, quartered
½ tsp each cumin, chives and rosemary
2 tsp oregano
pinch of turmeric
sea salt to taste
2 tsp cornflour

Cook peas and beans in salt water. In a deep pan, fry garlic in oil until brown. Add liver and cook for 2–3 minutes. Add all the other ingredients except the cornflour, and simmer for 30–35 minutes. Thicken with cornflour. Serve with brown rice cooked with a little turmeric, arranging as artistry dictates. Lovely for dinners on the terrace, if the evening midges allow!

DESERTS

Plas Newydd, at Llangollen, North Wales, is a delightful black-and-white house set in acres of lawns and evergreens – mostly hollies. The two eccentric ladies who lived there in the eighteenth century, Lady Eleanor Butler and the Hon. Sarah Parsonby, painlessly extracted tolls from their many friends who visited of holly seeds or other horticultural bits and pieces which they fancied. Come to think of it, most of my friends come bearing gifts for the garden . . .

This is really a gateau, but earned its name in our family because the youngest was always sent to 'dip' into the boot for it, when we reached the picnic site! We've enjoyed it on trips to Lincolnshire, Northamptonshire, the length and breadth of Wales, and many other places – many lovely memories.

Nice to eat 'on the hoof', in these sophisticated times, when the ice-box forms an essential part of one's impedimenta in the car boot.

Strawberry Dip

Serves 6
4 eggs
4 oz caster sugar
3 oz icing sugar
4 oz self-raising flour
salt to taste
2 tsp mint
¾ lb strawberries
½ pint double cream
whole mint leaves to decorate

In a deep bowl whisk eggs and both lots of sugar. Add flour and salt. Mix well, and spoon mixture into a non-stick sponge tin lined with whole mint leaves. Bake for 15 minutes at 375°F (190°C), Gas Mark 5. Allow to cool thoroughly.

Cut horizontally into two. Spread bottom half with half of strawberries and mint, and half the whipped cream. Add top layer of the dip, and spread likewise. Decorate with a few more mint leaves.

My mother was Yorkshire-born, so for us there's only one Richmond. Making the usual early start one day, we were looking round Richmond's twelfth-century Holy Trinity Church soon after nine o'clock. It was a lovely June day, the great door was open, and suddenly I heard a deep, throaty cough outside. Passing the gate was an elephant! We had a chat later with its keeper and discovered the road past Holy Trinity was close enough to Richmond Zoo to give the trunker his daily constitutional.

In the car that day, as on many other excursions, we enjoyed a fruit picnic. But, a warning: it's much better when you remember to pack the spoons.

Fruit Picnic

one raspberry jelly
one strawberry jelly
water
mixture of soft fruits, bananas, etc.
angelica leaves, chopped (or 1 tsp demerara sugar)
sprigs of mint to decorate

Make up the jellies, using enough water only for *one* between the two jellies. The added fruit provides its own liquid. I add no sugar but, if you haven't angelica, you might like a teaspoonful or so of demerara. Allow to set cold, and decorate with mint before locking in the ice-box of the car. Never use the ice-box to cool hot dishes.

For that fruity dish back at the base try

June Syllabub

Serves 6
1 ½ lb strawberries
2 fl oz brandy
3 oz caster sugar
½ pint double cream
¼ pint grape juice

Hull and wash the strawberries. Dry on absorbent paper. In a bowl, add brandy to the fruit and allow to meld overnight. Next day, stir in sugar. Whip cream until stiff. Mix grape juice into fruit and add fruit mixture gradually to cream, whisking the while. Spoon into sundae dishes and chill. Decorate with fruit of your choice: redcurrants are my favourite.

BREAD AND CAKES

In this season of colour – vegetable and fruit – it's a change to have a dark bread. Rye is fairly low in gluten and gives an awkward, sticky dough if used by itself; so mix and match your flours.

Rye Bread

Makes 3 loaves
1 ½ lb rye flour
1 ½ lb wholemeal flour
1 tbsp sea salt
4 oz butter
2 oz fresh yeast
warm water
sesame or caraway seeds to decorate

Make as for wholemeal bread (see January). Decorate with sesame or caraway seeds.

These are tailor-made for picnics – they've been with us to Grantham and Hereford (two chained libraries I find hard to leave), to Oxford and Birmingham, and on horticultural pilgrimages to Wisley and Levens.

Fruit Buns

Makes 24 buns
2 oz fresh yeast
6 oz demerara sugar
2 lb wholemeal flour
1 pint warm milk
salt to taste
4 oz sunflower margarine
4 eggs, beaten
6 oz sultanas
½ lb redcurrants
allspice to dust

In a large bowl, add yeast and 2 tsp sugar to 8 oz of the flour. Pour in warm milk and mix with wooden spoon. Set aside until frothy (30–40 minutes at room temperature). In another bowl, mix remainder of sugar, flour and salt. Melt margarine. Beat eggs. Into the yeast mixture, add margarine and eggs. Next add flour mixture and fruit. Knead the dough lightly in the bowl. Turn on to floured board, and work for 3–4 minutes.

Leave in a warmed bowl covered with a cloth, as for bread, for 2–3 hours. Re-knead lightly, and fill bun cases. Dust with allspice. Bake at 375°F (190°C), Gas Mark 5, for 15–20 minutes.

Picking strawberries used to give me a rash from wrists to elbows. I decided the leaves contained something which didn't like me. But I adore strawberries, so endured the rash. After some years, it went away: one of those unexplained allergies which resolve themselves.

In Hungary, they recommend keeping torte for 2 or 3 days in an airtight tin, to improve the flavour. In this house, we've still to be sufficiently strong-minded.

Strawberry Torte

Serves 6
4 eggs, separated
5 oz demerara sugar
4 oz fresh strawberries
Cream filling:
2 oz butter
2 oz icing sugar
1 tbsp instant coffee, dry powder
Topping:
3 oz caster sugar
1 tbsp water
9 strawberries to decorate

Grease two 7 in. sandwich tins. Whisk egg whites stiff. Whisk yolks with demerara sugar. Mix strawberries and whites into yolks. Divide mixture into tins and bake at 350°F (180°C), Gas Mark 4, for 30–35 minutes. Allow cakes to shrink slightly before turning them on to a wire tray to cool.

Prepare filling by creaming butter. Beat in icing sugar and coffee. Sandwich cooled cakes with this filling. For the topping, use a small saucepan to dissolve caster sugar in water. Bring to boil until syrup is golden. Pour this caramel over the torte, and add strawberry decoration while still warm.

June is a busy month, for something in one's psyche reacts to the long hours of daylight. If June lasted for twelve months, how exhausting it would be!

HERBS OF THE MONTH

Sweet Basil *Ocimum basilicum*
Half-hardy annual, to 8 in.

The name is thought to come from the Greek *basileus*, 'king'. Truly it is a herb fit for kings. It is said that basil was found growing near Christ's tomb after the resurrection. From Palestine it was taken to Greece, where in some Orthodox churches it is still used to prepare the holy water, and pots of basil are placed against the altar. In India it is known as *Tulasi*, sacred to the Hindu deities Krishna and Vishnu. A sprig of basil is often laid at a funeral on the body of a Hindu.

Don't chop the delicate leaves: tear them with the fingers, and add to sliced tomatoes, and green salads; tomato soup, zucchini (courgettes), peas and beans – all at the last minute before serving. Though delicate in constitution, basil has a strong pungent flavour which complements garlic. Basil freezes well, if the leaves are first coated on both sides with olive oil.

Use it freely to make the sauce beloved of Italians (who call it *Pesto*) and the Provençales (who call it *Pistou*): 4 oz basil leaves, 1 tbsp mildly roasted pine nuts, 2 large garlic cloves, 3 oz Parmesan cheese, 6 tbsp olive oil, salt and pepper. Pulp the basil, nuts and garlic, then add gradually the oil and cheese until the mix is creamy. Mix salt and pepper to taste, and stir into freshly cooked pasta.

A tonic can be made by steeping a few leaves in wine for several hours. As a cure for insomnia, infuse basil leaves as a tea and drink on going to bed.

In the garden grow basil well away from rue and sage. Site it, instead, among your tomatoes: the basil will thrive, and the tomatoes will not be troubled by white-fly. Pots of basil can be grown indoors on windowsills, where they will deter flies.

Alexanders *Smyrnium olusatrum*
Biennial, 3–4 ft

Theophrastus called this herb *Hipposelinon*, and in some areas today it's still known as 'horse parsley'. In the first century AD, Pliny and Columella praised its culinary virtues. In mediaeval times it was known as *Petroselinum alexandrinum*, the Rock Parsley of Alexandria, hence the modern name.

The black, aromatic seeds are used to flavour soups and stews, and give the plant another common name of 'Black Pot Herb'. They can also be ground and used sparingly as a condiment in dishes where pepper would otherwise be added. Shred the young leaves in salads and coleslaws. Mix them with watercress, chickweed, sweet cicely and nettles, and blend into chicken and garlic stock, for a nourishing early spring and summer soup. The flower buds can be added to salads. Boil the roots and serve with a white sauce – or crystallize them as a dessert.

Though the shoots have a pronounced angelica smell, this disappears in cooking.

Galen (AD 131–201), in medical terms probably second only to Hippocrates, compiled a herbal which was virtually unchallenged until the Middle Ages. In his treatment of alexanders he decided this herb's culinary virtues exceeded its medicinal worth. That may be true today, but in the meantime the seeds were used as an emmenagogue (being soaked in wine), and the dried leaves as an antiscorbutic on long sea-voyages, when Vitamin C was hard to come by. The antiseptic properties of the fresh juice can be effective in dressing small cuts and wounds.

Put the ripe seed through a coarse mincer and add for a piquant scent to *pot-pourris*. The fragrant, greeny-white flowers are stunning in arrangements, as also are the dried seed-heads.

On Britain's southern and western coastline, alexanders can at times be found growing wild. Cultivated, it's an exuberant, good-natured herb, and one of the first to be useable in the spring. A self-sower, once established from a first sowing, leaves will be pickable the following spring. Grow it in sun or partial shade. It's not really fussy as to soil, but doesn't like cold, wet conditions. The glossy green leaves usually push through the January snows, but the roots do best in sandy, free-draining soils.

Oregano *Origanum vulgare*
Fairly tender perennial, to 1 ft

Cooks have appreciated oregano since Roman times, when it was also valued as a symbol of peace and happiness. Growing 8–12 in. tall, with pink-through-to-magenta flowers, the name 'oregano' means 'mountain joy', and accurately describes its colourful abundance in Mediterranean climes.

For culinary purposes add fresh or dried leaves to sauces, soups, meat dishes and stuffings. In earlier times, Thé Rouge (oregano tisane) was used to flavour beer.

Today, oregano tea is used to relieve nervous headaches, stomach disorders and coughs. Tie a bunch of freshly-picked leaves in muslin and immerse in bathwater to alleviate rheumatic pains and general stiffness. For sufferers from insomnia, oregano as a hot or cold drink acts as a mild sedative. Try just a few leaves to a cupful of water, until you've grown accustomed to the flavour.

The flowers are useful and long-lasting in tussie-mussies and arrangements of all kinds, particularly when sited in a hallway or porch where they can be brushed in passing to release their strong aroma.

Oregano loves the sunny warmth of its native Italy, so pamper it a little; it's worth the trouble, for its distinctive, sharp flavour. The sunniest, warmest place in your garden will bring out its pungency. Be prepared to re-sow each spring. Oregano in Britain dies down completely in the autumn, but our fairly damp winters are more injurious than the dry cold of mountain slopes further south. Recently, however, this herb's increasing popularity has seen acres of it being sown commercially in North America, using hardier strains from Himalayan regions, growing at altitudes as high as 2,000 metres.

Fennel *Foeniculum vulgare*
Hardy biennial or perennial, to 5 ft

For over 2,000 years the varied benefits of fennel have been recognized. In Roman times men ate it to keep fit, and ladies to keep slender. Our Anglo-Saxon forebears held it sacred as a power against evil. Its medicinal properties ensured a generous bed of fennel in every monastery garden. Nicholas Culpeper, the seventeenth-century herbalist, observed that fennel seed 'boiled in wine and drunk is good for those that are bitten with serpents, or have eaten poisonfull herbs or mushrooms.' And Longfellow has immortalized in poetry its strength-giving quality: 'So gladiators fierce and rude/mingled it with their daily food/and he who battled and subdued/a wreath of fennel wore'.

Fennel is so pungent usually only the young foliage is used in the kitchen. Sprinkle a few of the threadlike leaves on, or inside, fish; also with meat dishes, soups, stews, salads and in sauces. I like a pinch in natural yoghurt. Half-ripe seed, produced in generous umbels, is tasty pickled with gherkins and cucumbers. Use ripe seeds in biscuits and bread – but sparingly. The roots and stems can be gently steamed as a vegetable, but serve in small portions, as large amounts of fennel can react adversely on the nervous system.

Yet, in moderation, fennel is an excellent digestive and intestinal disinfectant. It's used today to flavour many otherwise unpalatable medicines, and also in toothpastes. Flatulence can be relieved with fennel tea: infuse 1 tsp of ripe seeds in ½ pint boiling water. Take in small doses.

A hard winter can kill this useful herb, but usually self-sown seedlings survive. In any case, save some of the seed to sow in spring for fennel is at best a short-lived perennial, becoming woody after three or four years. Choose a well-drained, sunny site – at the foot of a wall is ideal – where it will get some protection and not become waterlogged. Keep it well away from dill; cross-pollination can alter the piquant flavour of both herbs.

July

Berry pudding
July

---

*Trust in the Lord, and do good; so shalt thou dwell
in the land, and verily thou shalt be fed. Delight
thyself also in the Lord, and he shall give thee the
desires of thine heart.*
(Psalm 37:3, 4)

July

STARTERS

Chervil Soup • Salad Kebabs • Asparagus Pea Dip

SAVOURY LIGHT LUNCHEON/
SUPPER DISHES

Summer Ratatouille • Sausage Snack
• Cheese and Courgette Pie •

DINNER (MAIN COURSE DISHES)

Trout with Lovage • Beef and Melting Moments
• Liver and Scorzonera •

DESSERTS

Blackcurrant Cheesecake
• Peaches and Herb Ice Cream • Chervil Caramel •

BREAD AND CAKES

Sunflower Loaf • Summer Victoria • Berry Pudding

HERBS OF THE MONTH

Lovage • Chervil • Borage • Roman Chamomile

Except where otherwise stated, each recipe caters for four people

---

However large one's variety of vegetables, some garden space should always be earmarked for new potatoes. Tubers scuffed prematurely out of the compost and rushed to the kitchen need only a brief rinse under the tap, before meeting boiling salted water for 3–4 minutes. Melting moments, they are, and worth all the time and space they take up: the chitting in trays in February, planting in March gales or blizzards on Good Friday, earthing-up to beat the April frosts . . .

STARTERS

Summer soups here are almost always eaten hot – for in the Peak District the weather is never too hot for hot soup.

Chervil Soup

Serves 6
2 oz butter
salt and pepper to taste
½ pint apple juice
1 ½ pints chicken stock
4 oz chervil
½ pint double cream

In a deep pan melt butter. Add seasoning, juice and stock. Stir in chervil. Bring to boil, cover and allow to simmer for 20–25 minutes. Stir in cream the last 2 minutes before serving. A quick, easy and deliciously different soup.

It's July when an army of fruit-harvesters moves in – friends with no gardens of their own, but with other skills to barter for the pleasure of picking and taking home fresh fruit. It's a lovely time, and the canes and bushes benefit from the minimum of fruit being allowed to remain. A favourite with my army is

Salad Kebabs

Very simply, thread on long skewers any thing to hand: radishes, cucumbers, tomatoes, mange-touts, lettuce, melon, potato fries, mushrooms, raw or cooked carrot, prawns, ham, chicken, beef slices, various cheeses . . . Aim for as much colour as possible. There's a unique, quite un-British appeal in eating things off a skewer.

The first time we grew asparagus peas they were all minus and no plus: the plants flopped about in summer gales, the peas were fiddly to prepare, and 80 per cent of the crop out-paced us and grew stringy.

Their second season saw quite the reverse: we had few winds, so the bed stayed tidy; the mahogany-coloured flowers were seen to advantage. Because the weather was dry for much of the summer, the papery sheath at the end of each pod dropped away of its own volition; and the dryness encouraged regular picking of inch-long, tender pods. So now we grow them every year.

Asparagus Pea Dip

Simply boil the wee, winged pods for 7–10 minutes, blend into soft curd cheese, and serve as a dip with crispy potato fries, or as a spread. Don't be tempted to add flavourings as the delicate asparagus taste will be lost.

LIGHT SAVOURY DISHES

While my father was alive we visited Newstead Abbey, once the home of Lord Byron. We saw the monument to 'Bo'sun', his dog, and the ruins of the abbey against the house. They called him 'Vee-ron' in Greece, where he loved to stay. We ate ratatouille on this ancient site, and thought of the man who never seemed to find his niche . . .

Summer Ratatouille

Serves 6
6 tomatoes
2 aubergines
2 courgettes
1 clove garlic
2 oz broad beans
2 oz runner or French beans
2 oz peas
6 tbsp olive oil
pinches of chamomile, lovage, mint
and thyme
salt to taste

Prepare the vegetables, dicing as small or as large as you prefer. In a deep pan heat the oil and add all ingredients. Cover, and simmer for 30–35 minutes, stirring occasionally. Can be enjoyed hot in winter, cold in summer. Don't stick to my recipe – be daring, and inventive! Mine is never the same twice over.

These sausages started life here by mistake. The day had been stormy and for much of the time we'd been without electricity. Too busy to motor into town, I'd taken the line of least resistance and delved into the freezer for cod steaks, only the fish turned out to be sausages. Late in the evening power was restored, and a new dish concocted which has graced the table on many subsequent occasions.

Sausage Snack

Serves 6
12 herb sausages
olive oil
1 garlic clove, chopped
4 tbsp borage leaves, chopped
sea salt
6 leeks
borage flowers

Fry the sausages in a little oil. Add chopped garlic and borage, with seasoning. Boil the leeks (far too small to be picked with a clear conscience in July, but deliciously tender) in next to no water. Serve with baked potatoes garnished with pinky-blue borage flowers (having first removed the black hairy calyxes).

I grow masses of courgettes: some we give away to friends, the rest are eaten raw or cooked. I'm not among the ranks of those who like them frozen. Grown in the tomato house, the plants look like triffids come September. One or two fruits always escape attention, and end up as marrows at Harvest Festival.

Cheese and Courgette Pie

Serves 6
8 oz shortcrust pastry (prepared)
8 oz white Cheshire cheese, grated
4 courgettes, sliced
1 clove garlic, chopped
salt and pepper to taste
little oil

Using a 7 in. pie dish, halve the prepared pastry. Line the dish with one half. Cover with cheese and finely-sliced courgettes. Chop garlic and sprinkle over, with seasoning. Top with the rest of the pastry, crimping the edges together. Brush with oil and prick or slit for ventilation in the pastry top. Bake at 400°F (200°C), Gas Mark 6, for 30–35 minutes.

MAIN COURSE DISHES

---

*July is the time when a few of my friends vanish to some corner
of a foreign field, and I think how fortunate I am to be staying
at home. The dahlias – my favourite flowers – are turning part
of the vegetable garden into a riot of colour, and need hours of
tying-in, dead-heading and general T.L.C. Each season brings
its own delights: from the demure, pristine whiteness of
February's 'Fair Maids'; through April's daffodil-gold; and the
extravagance of June poppies; to the vividness of July's dahlias,
so uncompromisingly determined in their effort to dazzle. It's
worth the effort of bringing them on early, to have four or five
months of sheer exuberance.*

*Many friends who haven't gone in search of Egypt's lotus
or Italy's bougainvillea come round just to see the dahlias
and stay for*

Trout with Lovage

4 trout, prepared
wholemeal flour
2 tbsp lovage
butter
salt and white pepper
olive oil

Coat the fish with flour. Pack each with
lovage, dotted with knobs of butter. Season,
and fry in a little oil, allowing 5 minutes a side.
Serve with Basmati rice or wholemeal bread
fresh from the oven.

My mother grew up not far from the Derbyshire-Yorkshire border. It was a large house, and my grandmother had a French cook. While she often bemoaned the state of the kitchen floor, his cooking was irreproachable, though my mother – as a child – was often prevailed upon to make the sauces.

In that valley, several weeks earlier than this garden, fresh potatoes and green peas were to be had early in June. Here we're still enjoying 'melting moments' throughout July – except, towards the end of the month, the potatoes need an extra 2–3 minutes' cooking.

Beef and Melting Moments

Serves 4
2 lb steak fillets
sunflower margarine
½ tsp each of chamomile, sage, rosemary and thyme
salt and pepper to taste
new potatoes
green peas
flour to thicken

The new potatoes should be freshly dug, if possible, and the green peas should be picked quickly and rushed to the kitchen. I don't coat the meat in flour. Fry quickly in margarine, adding the finely-shredded herbs and seasoning. Cook potatoes in unsalted water to preserve their fresh 'earthiness'. The peas can be podded and cooked for 2 minutes only, or picked very young and served as mange-touts (again, cook only for 2–3 minutes). Thicken the beef juices with a little flour, and serve as gravy.

I love both salsify and scorzonera, and always see them as twins – a bit like scillas and chionodoxas, those blue beauties of spring. (If scorzonera is not available, use parsnips – or even carrots if parsnips are out of season.) Why so many cooks like to skin scorzonera, I've never fathomed. I was always taught that with most vegetables and fruit much of the goodness is either in the skin, or just below it; and these days one hears a lot about the value of roughage.

Liver and Scorzonera

Serves 6
6 scorzonera roots, sliced
water to cook
3 lb pigs liver
olive oil
1 tsp chervil
1 tsp basil
1 garlic clove, chopped
sea salt

Scrub the scorzonera, cut into slices and cook in unsalted water. Bring to boil and simmer for 7–10 minutes. Fry the liver in a very little oil, with herbs and seasoning. Serve, spooning the herby juice over the scorzonera. Duchesse potatoes are an optional extra: I like the scorzonera as the only vegetable.

DESSERTS

I've always admired those people who could do two jobs at once. When I'm writing, mealtimes vary according to inspiration. But the domestic chaos would be infinitely worse without Emma, our dog, and the cats, who exercise great ingenuity and sometimes force majeure *to remind me of the need to dish up food of sorts at somewhat regular times. It was the delightfully witty Frank Muir, also a cat-lover, who once remarked in the course of* My Word *that he was sure cats thought they needed feeding every eighteen minutes. The only disadvantage with this month's first dessert is that its cook is tempted to help herself to a piece every eighteen minutes.*

Blackcurrant Cheesecake

Serves 6 (in theory)
6 oz digestive biscuits
3 ½ oz butter
2 oz caster sugar
sprinkling of lavender flowers
The filling:
1 blackcurrant jelly
8 oz soft curd cheese
2 oz caster sugar
¼ lb blackcurrants
The topping:
1 oz demerara sugar
butter to mix
½ oz ground almonds

Crush biscuits with a rolling pin in a polythene bag. In a pan melt butter. Add sugar and lavender to the biscuit crumbs. Blend into the butter, and turn out to line a pie dish. Press firmly. Make up the jelly and set aside to cool. Cream cheese and sugar. Add fruit, and whisk in the jelly. Spoon on to the biscuit base and chill. For the topping, cream sugar with a little butter. Whisk in the ground almond and spread on the filling.

Peaches and Herb Ice Cream

Not really a recipe, for all I do is pick the peaches, warm with the sun, quarter them to extract the stones (never, never skin fresh peaches), and ladle soft ice cream greened with extra-finely chopped spearmint. Exquisite!

We had something like this dessert when I visited Paris – only there they used mint with the orange, instead of chervil. Sometimes I make it with mint, for memory's sake.

Chervil Caramel

rind of 1 orange
½ pint orange juice
2 tbsp cold water
4 oz caster sugar
3 eggs
3 egg yolks
1½ tbsp demerara sugar
3 tsp chervil, chopped

Grate orange rind and steep in juice, preferably overnight, but at the very least for 2 hours. Warm four dariole moulds. In a small pan pour cold water over caster sugar, and stir well. Bring to boil until golden. Divide this caramel between the moulds, and agitate moulds (protect hands with gloves) until the inner surface is coated evenly.

Over low heat, warm juice and rind. Whisk eggs and all yolks with demerara sugar to a cream. Pour near-boiling juice on to the eggs and stir in. Add chervil gradually, stirring the while. Fill up the dariole moulds and stand in 1 in. hot water in a roasting dish. Cover with foil and bake at 350°F (180°C), Gas Mark 4, for 25–30 minutes. Cool and chill on a stone bench or in the fridge. To serve, turn out from moulds and decorate with raspberry ice cream.

Oh, to be in Russia for morozhenoye! *When Sir Winston Churchill visited Moscow, and saw the queues outside the ubiquitous ice cream kiosks, he is reputed to have exclaimed: 'In all this snow! These people will never be conquered!'*

The Russians make ice cream in more flavours than a well-known firm's '57', but the one I loved best was the apricot morozhenoye *we had with coffee – the tastiest, strongest coffee St Petersburg could offer, served in pretty glasses set in silver filigree, the generous wodge of ice cream slowly melting black into* café au lait. *Sometimes I serve ice cream in coffee here – but it's not the same.*

BREAD AND CAKES

Sunflowers: aren't they gorgeous, those 12 ft, nodding dinner-plates of chocolate brown and yellow? Ever since the day I sat, pen poised, at the library desk entranced with the ecstasy of blue-and great-tits attacking a giant sunflower's seeds in a terrace bed, I've grown this obliging annual – just for the birds. I buy my sunflower seeds for

Sunflower Loaf

This recipe is my well-proven wholemeal bread (see January), with the addition of 4 oz sunflower seeds, ground or chopped, to each 1 lb of flour. I add 30 minutes to the normal proving time.

When my mother was alive we had a solid-fuel Aga, as well as the electric stove. But even an Aga acknowledges the passing of time. I still miss it: sponge cakes were spongier . . . No, I mustn't blame the stove for the results. This always reminds me of a jingle my father used to quote:

> *'If I make mistakes in spelling,
> Molly dear,' said he,
> 'Remember it's the pen that's bad –
> Don't lay the blame on me!'*

So I work hard on my

Summer Victoria

4 oz butter
4 oz demerara sugar
2 eggs
½ tsp each orange mint, eau-de-cologne mint and eucalyptus mint
½ tsp nutmeg
4 oz self-raising flour

I use two non-stick 7 in. tins. In a bowl cream butter and sugar. Beat in eggs and add herbs and nutmeg. Gradually add flour and beat well. Divide mixture into the tins and bake side by side (if possible) at 350°F (180°C), Gas Mark 4, for 20–25 minutes. Cool on a wire tray.

I like crushed fresh raspberries as a layer-filling, but redcurrants add a nice tang. Decorate the top with puréed strawberries and eat as soon as possible. If the fruit seeps into the sponge, cut your losses and use the cake as the base for a super trifle!

This recipe is based on the Olde English Summer Pudding, and the more fruits that can be used, the better.

Berry Pudding

Serves 6
½ tsp French sorrel
8 slices wholemeal bread, toast thickness
½ lb each of strawberries, raspberries, redcurrants
4 oz demerara sugar
½ tsp lemon verbena

Soak the sorrel for 1 hour, to extract oxalic acid. Drain on absorbent paper. Line a pudding basin with 6 slices of bread. In a wide pan bring to the boil fruit and sugar. Cook for 2–3 minutes, and add herbs. Pour into basin and top with remainder of bread. Cover with weighted plate and leave – if you can – for a day, until the juices and flavours have impregnated all the bread. Turn out and serve with lashings of cream.

The end of July brings a noticeable shortening of the late evening daylight, however hard one tries not to notice. But the blackcurrant bushes, stripped of fruit, are pleading to be pruned, and already one needs to look forward to another year's harvest.

HERBS OF THE MONTH

Lovage *(Levisticum officinale,* 'Love Parsley')
Hardy perennial, to 6 ft

Once considered an aphrodisiac, the name outlived its reputation. The Greeks and Romans used lovage in the kitchen and the bath, practices followed later by our Tudors and Stuarts. The digestive properties were promoted by Benedictine monks in mediaeval times. More prosaically, they also used the leaves to line their sandals on journeys between monasteries, and during the hours of traversing stone passages and steps on their home ground.

From its roots upwards lovage is edible, with a unique yeasty flavour. Use the young shoots as celery, in soups, stews and sauces. The young leaves can be torn into salads, and cooked with poultry and in casseroles. Lovage, unlike many herbs, is added at the start of cooking. Dry the leaves for winter use. Boil the roots and serve either with oil and vinegar, or puréed with a cheese sauce. The dried seeds can be used to flavour soups, especially tomato and mushroom, and stews; or crushed in breads and biscuits.

Chew the seeds to help digestion. An even tastier remedy is made by steeping fresh seeds in brandy and adding a dash of sugar. Add the dried, powdered root to bathwater as a skin tonic. Our forebears used lovage for circulatory ills and to treat the kidneys. Nowadays, kidney sufferers are not recommended to use this herb without professional advice. However, a mild infusion of leaves, seeds or roots can reduce fever and is good for delayed or painful menstruation. Avoid lovage when pregnant.

This herb makes a handsome, free-standing plant for the back of a border. In spring, attractive coppery shoots grow out into bright-green, celerylike leaves which expand as the year progresses, to 2½ ft across. Umbels of lime-green to yellow flowers give way to pretty, brown winged seeds. Lovage likes a rich, moisture-retentive soil and a position in full sun.

Chervil *(Anthriscus cerefolium)*
Hardy annual or biennial, to 2½ ft

This herb was traditionally eaten as a pick-me-up after the Lenten fast, on Maundy Thursday. Often one's introduction to chervil comes when holidaying in France, the country which has long been the prime appreciator and user of this herb. However, once it's refreshing anise taste has been acquired, you'll want to grow it at home.

Chervil wilts quickly so it needs to be added to hot dishes (soups, omelettes, casseroles) only a minute or two before serving. Chervil is a vital ingredient of Omelette Fines Herbes – a blend of chives, parsley, chervil and tarragon. Keep at least a bag of each of these herbs in the freezer for all-the-year-round use. Despite its frail appearance, chervil freezes well. Don't forget to label the bags: its spicy, aniseed, parsley-like flavour tinged with myrrh, is not the answer to every dish!

To savour chervil at its best, eat it raw in salads – or garnish fish with chervil butter. Use salted butter for the best result: soften, and beat in 2 or 3 tbsp torn – not chopped – chervil to ½ lb butter. Keep fairly cool, but not refrigerated, for 2 hours, allowing the flavour of the herb to penetrate the butter. Fridge for 5 minutes maximum, then serve.

Add a few leaves to vinegar, or use chervil in a fish sauce: simply add seasoning to fresh cream, then with a generous hand mix in torn chervil leaves *gently* – a blender will give you a pretty green sauce, but sacrifices much of the flavour of the herb in so doing. Finally, try this tasty salad dressing: natural yoghurt, a dash of lemon juice, sea salt, and a mixture of chervil, parsley and chives. Play around with the quantities, until you achieve the taste you like.

I've mentioned the restorative qualities of chervil, in its traditional Maundy Thursday connection, on p. 000. It's also a good source of iron, magnesium, carotene and Vitamin C (best eaten raw to get the full benefit from these).

Chervil tea (1 tbsp per cup boiling water, allow to infuse for 10–12 minutes) helps the digestion and has been used to treat catarrh, disorders of the liver and arthritis. The bruised fresh stems and leaves, when applied to wounds, aid healing.

Chervil adapts well to windowbox culture, or in pots in the kitchen. Chervil's a quick grower: start cutting the delicate leaves 6–8 weeks after sowing. Given cold greenhouse protection in the winter, plants started outdoors will give a second cutting or two the following spring.

Borage (*Borago officinalis,* 'Bee Borage')
Hardy annual, to 2½ ft

Borage has been known since the days of Pliny as a herb for chasing away the blues and promoting happiness. It was the basis of Homer's *nepenthe* wine, which carried bliss into oblivion. We find its cheery, clear-blue or pinky flowers smiling up at us from mediaeval tapestries, from the Virgin's robes in Old Masters' paintings, and from the elaborately tooled Books of Hours and ancient herbals. In Crusading times, borage flowers were added to wine to bolster the courage of knights riding to battle.

Pick the star-shaped flowers, carefully removing the hairy black calyx, and use them for colouring salads, fruit dishes and ice cream. Chopped young leaves make cold drinks colder. In salads, like the flowers, they add a cucumber taste. If the leaves are cooked in soups, and with any of the brassica tribe, there's less or no need to add salt. Chopped, they enhance soft cream cheeses, and add an interesting flavour to ravioli stuffing. The flowers can be crystallized, and used through the winter, being especially pretty on Christmas jellies and desserts.

The Crusaders discovered what modern science is now confirming: that this herb's high percentage of nitrate of potassium, calcium and mineral salts acts on the adrenal gland. Borage is, in fact, recommended for those on a salt-free diet.

Drunk as a tea, it can alleviate kidney and bladder disorders, and rheumatism.

Many borage plants bear pink flowers among the blue, as summer advances. Bees flock to borage flowers: grow this herb near strawberries and tomatoes and your fruits will be better pollinated, and the pests of these plants kept at bay. The seed keeps fresh for several years; but once you've introduced borage to your garden, it will usually self-sow with audacious fervour.

Roman Chamomile *Anthemis nobile*
(Syn. *Chamaemelum nobile*)
Creeping perennial, to 6 in.
Single and double-flowered forms available.

In ancient Egypt chamomile was dedicated to the sun because it cured agues. The Greeks knew it as 'Earth Apple', from its fruity aroma. Chamomile is included in the Nine Sacred Herbs of an Anglo-Saxon manuscript, the *Lacnunga*. Mediaeval gardens sometimes incorporated chamomile seats, but generally it was planted on walking areas. 'The more it is trodden on, the faster it grows,' says Falstaff in Shakespeare's *Henry IV, Part I* (II.iv.388). Indoors, it was a popular strewing herb. It is not recorded as being among the herbs taken to America by the Pilgrim Fathers but it reached New Jersey fairly soon afterwards, and was quickly hailed as an ideal gastric and insomnia cure.

Chamomile flowers and leaves can be used in *pot-pourris* and (often with other herbs) in pillows. The whole herb is used in the making of beer. The main culinary uses of chamomile is as a tea, a general tonic (put the flowers, 1 oz dried, or a handful of fresh, into a heatproof jug – neither copper nor aluminium. Pour in 1 pint boiling water. Allow to stand for 8–10 minutes).

The herbalist Parkinson once wrote: 'Chamomile is put to divers and sundry uses, both for pleasure and profit, both for the sick and the sound, in bathing to comfort and strengthen the sound, and to ease pain in the diseased.'

An infusion of the flowers makes a good skin tonic, and can whiten coarse skin. Used cold, as a tea bag compress, it reduces inflammation of the eyes. Collect and dry the flowers when young. They are a disinfectant and antiseptic: chew them to ease toothache. Use an infusion to treat burns and swellings; as a general tonic; and in the bathwater to give relief to a variety of aches and pains. Make a rinse for blonde hair, for chamomile acts as a mild bleach: use 6 oz of fresh chamomile to 1 pint water; infuse for 30 minutes, and use warm. Wipe leaves on the skin as an insect-repellent.

If you don't have the space for a chamomile lawn or path at least plant it along the front of a border, where it can be brushed in passing. It likes light, fairly poor soil and tolerates a fair amount of drought. When cold chamomile tea is sprayed on seedlings it deters damping-off. Plants in the vicinity of chamomile are kept free of pests and diseases, and on the compost heap it promotes decomposition. Truly, a gardener's friend!

August

the Flower Festival —
August

The earth which drinketh in the rain that cometh
oft upon it, and bringeth forth herbs meet for them
by whom it is dressed, receiveth blessing from God.
(Hebrews 6:7)

August

STARTERS

Soupe Maritime • Crispes aux Herbes
• Stuffed Avocadoes •

SAVOURY LIGHT LUNCHEON/
SUPPER DISHES

Courgette Salad • Herby Yorkshire Pudding
• Skirret aux Pois •

DINNER (MAIN COURSE DISHES)

Shepherd's Pie • Chicken with Crosnes
• Salmon au Chine •

DESSERTS

Rhubarb and Angelica Pancakes • Plum Pie
• Festival Trifle •

BREAD AND CAKES

Oatey Bread • Festival Buns • Apple Loaf

HERBS OF THE MONTH

Egyptian Onion • Skirret • Angelica • Mullein

Except where otherwise stated, each recipe caters for four people

---

One of my favourite festivals is that of the Transfiguration (6 August), perhaps because it's not been commercialized like some of the larger feasts. The garden is at its colourful best then, and most of the soft fruit is safely frozen or bottled (or eaten). Those friends who haven't taken the children to the Costa del Blackpool come over for more relaxing evenings than have been possible since May. We know we'll have to leave the peace of the mountain and go back to the bustle of the plain, but that's not for at least a fortnight!

STARTERS

This soup takes me back to the one and only time I went to Blackpool: four days midweek in August 1953. I'd just fallen off a pony and badly broken my arm, which was probably the reason I didn't want to go on another holiday for nearly twenty years. But the soup was good. I can enjoy it now without hearing the monotonous drone of the sea, or tasting the sharp salty spray thrown across the prom by waves higher than I'd thought could be.

Soupe Maritime

Serves 6
1 clove garlic, chopped
6 tbsp olive oil
1 cucumber, sliced
2 lb cod, cooked and flaked
1 bay leaf
1 ½ pints fish stock
¼ pint white wine
1 tbsp fennel
sea salt to taste
¼ pint double cream

In a deep pan fry garlic in oil until translucent. Add thinly sliced cucumber (not skinned or de-seeded, as there's goodness all through). Add cod flakes, bay, stock, wine and fennel and stir over a medium heat for 5–10 minutes. Add seasoning and cream, but don't allow to boil.

I've tried this with raw fish, but prefer it pre-cooked: it saves so much time on the day! If you've a blender, then blend; we like the chunkiness of the unliquidized soup.

When the five-day Flower Festival at our local church is in full swing (over the Bank Holiday weekend), saving time in the kitchen is a priority. This recipe wouldn't do a lot for one's figure if eaten at a normal time – but organizing a Flower Festival devours the calories.

Crispes aux Herbes

Make in batches for as many guests as you think may come.

a feast of herbs – mix and match
olive oil
6 potatoes, waxy not floury

Crumble or chop herbs finely, and in a deep pan add to oil. Wash, peel and thinly slice potatoes. Fry for 3–5 minutes until golden on both sides. Save the herby oil for flavouring other dishes. Serve crispes hot or cold – they disappear unbelievably quickly in either case.

For a long time I sheered off these delicious pears because I hadn't sufficient heat to grow them. Then one day I was lunching in Piccadilly – the London one. In the famous restaurant opposite St James's Church we had the most delicious avocadoes, and I was convinced of their charms on the spot. I remember, too, the thrill I had afterwards of seeing an Indian Bean Tree (Catalpa bignonioides) in full bean in St James's Churchyard. So it's only natural I always use runner beans in this recipe!

Stuffed Avocadoes

Serves 6
6 oz runner beans
3 avocado pears
8 oz prawns, peeled
2 tbsp double cream
2 tbsp natural yoghurt
1 tsp parsley
cucumber to garnish

Use the tiniest most tender beans possible. Cook the beans for a mere 2–3 minutes. Drain and cool. Cut each avocado in half, scoop out the flesh, keeping the stones to one side (children love to start these into growth – so do many not so young). Mix the flesh with the beans and the rest of the ingredients to the consistency you choose: I like a fairly rough texture. Return to the pear skins, and decorate with a twirled cucumber slice or two.

LIGHT SAVOURY DISHES

When we went to Melbourne (in Derbyshire), I was intrigued with the bird-cage, a wrought-iron summerhouse overlooking the lake. It was a beautiful day: in the photograph I took of my parents at the summerhouse, my mother's wearing a pretty blue and white frock – and you don't wear summer frocks too often in Derbyshire. On the way we stopped for a picnic and Mother's salad – designed to last for the homeward trip as well – disappeared to the last tomato seed.

Courgette Salad

There could be no garlic or chives in this – members of the allium family were not allowed within scenting distance of Mother. I've inherited her aversion to onions, but dearly love garlic and leeks and tolerate chives.

Serves 6 (in theory)
1 lb baby courgette, 3–5 in. only, sliced
3 butterhead lettuce hearts, shredded
6 red tomatoes, sliced
6 yellow tomatoes, sliced
sprigs of parsley, thyme, mint and any other herbs
6 hard-boiled eggs, sliced
1 cucumber, sliced
¼ lb petits pois
a very little horseradish, grated

Combine all the ingredients in a bowl and toss. Sealed with clingfilm in the cold-box of your car boot, this salad travels well but never makes it back to base.

As I've mentioned, my mother was Yorkshire-born. For all of us, there's a time when we make our first Yorkshire Pudding. She was quite young, and her parents stoically ate every mouthful. Not a comment was made until later that afternoon, when a visitor called. My grandfather asked innocently, had he met an elephant up the road? No, replied the visitor, perplexed. 'A pity,' said Grandfather, straight-faced, not meeting Mother's eye. 'We've just had a leather waistcoat for luncheon. He might have found it useful.'

Years later, when Mother's Yorkshire Pudds were the envy of her friends, she could laugh about that first attempt. Mine are nothing like hers – but then, I was only born in Derbyshire. I do, though, follow the Yorkshire custom of eating this recipe as a dish in its own right.

Herby Yorkshire Pudding

4 oz strong plain flour
sea salt to taste
1 egg
½ pint milk
½ tsp each thyme, burnet and rocket
¼ tsp sage
1 oz sunflower margarine

Into a bowl sift flour and salt. Fold in the egg gently with a wooden spoon. Gradually add the milk and herbs. Set aside for 3–4 hours.

In a baking tin, heat the margarine near the top of the oven, at 425°F (220°C), Gas Mark 7, until it begins to smoke. Pour in the batter and bake for 35–40 minutes. Avoid opening the oven door while the pudding is baking. I usually serve this with a dish of horseradish relish.

Mange-tout peas are so worthwhile. The French make pea-pod soup, but in Britain millions of pods of ordinary peas are thrown away – or at best added to compost heaps. However with mange-tout one feels, virtuously, nothing is going to waste.

Skirret, which is deservedly making something of a comeback, is lovely with peas – and still unusual enough to intrigue guests.

Skirret aux Pois

Serves 6
12 roots skirret
¼ lb mange-tout
¼ lb petits pois
1 tsp mixed coriander and oregano
Sauce:
2 tbsp cornflour
½ pint milk
knob of butter
salt to taste
pinch of thyme

Wash and scrub skirret. Cut into slivers and boil with the peas and herbs for 5–7 minutes. (Allow a little longer if not fresh).

The sauce is a simple white thyme sauce. Mix cornflour to a paste with a little of the milk. Boil remainder of milk. Add blended cornflour. Stir well and bring to the boil again. Add butter, seasoning and thyme. Stir continuously until it thickens. Serve with the skirret and peas.

MAIN COURSE DISHES

Being a farmer's daughter, Shepherd's Pie was never Cottage Pie in our house, though I have to admit the Cottage Pie of school luncheons was the only dish which redeemed those menus from the commonplace. I'm reliably informed school meals have made great strides since the fifties. This dish – whatever one calls it – never loses its appeal.

Shepherd's Pie

Serves 6

1 clove garlic, chopped
3 oz sunflower margarine
¾ lb minced beef, cooked
4 fl oz beef stock
salt to taste
pinches each of thyme and rosemary
2 bay leaves
½ oz broad beans
½ oz runner beans
½ oz peas
½ oz cauliflower florets
¾ oz mushrooms, sliced
½ oz courgettes, diced
2–3 tbsp milk
1 lb floury potatoes, mashed

In a deep pan, fry garlic in a little margarine until golden. Add meat and heat until slightly brown. Add stock, seasoning, herbs and vegetables. Simmer, while beating remaining (melted) margarine and milk into potatoes.

Into a deep pie or roasting dish, spoon meat and vegetables. Top with potato (I don't ripple the top, as many do). Bake at 425°F (220°C), Gas Mark 7, for 25–30 minutes, when the potatoes should be just browning. Delicious hot or cold.

Crosnes (Chinese artichokes) are so delicious, but fiddly enough not to be popular. Ours have their own patch up at the south end of the vegetable garden – for however conscientiously one digs them, some wee tubers will always hide and surprise you next spring. The purple flowers are a cross between toadflax and hyssop. The quaintly curled tubers need immediate washing, or grit stays in their crevices like honey on a bear's paw. Young crosnes are nice nibbled raw.

Chicken with Crosnes

Treat yourself to a tender 2½ lb chicken (or more of the same size, according to the number of diners), and stuff the body cavity with crosnes. No salt, no garlic – just crosnes. In a deep covered pan, add water to the level of the breastbone, and bring to the boil. Simmer, allowing 1 hour to each pound of meat. Serve with unbuttered, unseasoned baked potatoes.

One of Mother's cousins was a missionary in China in the 1890s. I still have some of the lovely blue and white cross-stitched bags she brought back, and her redwood chop-sticks, which I've never mastered. Luckily this dish tastes a treat using knives and forks. Actually, this sweet-and-sour recipe is based on a German dish: cookery knows few boundaries.

Salmon au Chine

Serves 6
Sauce:
5 tbsp olive oil
2 tbsp cider vinegar
2 cloves garlic or 2 Egyptian onion bulbs, crushed
4 red tomatoes, pounded
1 tbsp clear honey
½ tsp coriander
½ tsp cumin
1 tbsp black mustard powder
pinch of nutmeg
sea salt

6 salmon steaks, fresh or tinned
1 courgette to garnish

Mix the sauce ingredients and set aside for 2 hours to meld. Arrange salmon steaks on a fish plate, top with sauce, and decorate with slivers of young courgette.

DESSERTS

Originally I timed the Flower Festival to coincide with the peak of the dahlia season. Happily, it's also a very fruitful period, so we live on fresh desserts. Before I cottoned-on to Flower Festivals, I held our Church Garden Party here in August – but after two consecutive rainy events when 500 teas had to be served indoors, the appeal of flowers in the church grew irresistible.

Pancakes in August? Yes, but with a difference. Mother's great-grandmother having been a Fraser of Inverness, I not only wear the dress Fraser kilt on occasion, but am also hooked on these Scotch pancakes (Drop Scones, if you hail from 'South o' the Border'.)

Rhubarb and Angelica Pancakes

4 oz self-raising flour
2 tbsp demerara sugar
1 egg
¼ pint milk
2 tsp lemon balm
olive oil
2 lb rhubarb, chopped
2 tsp demerara sugar
2 tsp angelica, chopped

I use a heavy, non-stick frying pan, when the girdle plate is in use at the Festival. Mix flour and sugar in a bowl. Beat in the egg and half the milk. Add crumbled or finely-chopped balm, with the remainder of the milk. Beat well.

Heat a very little oil in the pan, until it begins to smoke. Pour in a spoonful of mixture, and brown on both sides. Keep each pancake warm on the grill shelf, until all are done. Meanwhile, stew rhubarb, sugar and angelica. Serve the rhubarb piping hot, on top of the pancakes, with swirls of ice cream.

Flower Festival time is plum time. I don't grow any here but dear friends, appreciating my preoccupation with the Festival, come bearing gifts of red plums, yellow plums, raw plums, cooked plums and plum jam. Together we demolish these delicious fruits of August.

Plum Pie

I ring the changes with pastry, made in the halcyon, lazy days of, well, pre-Festival. Plums are lovely with such a variety of pie pastries – it's hard to choose between shortcrust, American crust, rich flan and rough puff. Very few plums need added sugar. I like a pinch of nutmeg as a topping to the ice cream I invariably serve with the pie (saves making custard!). Whatever did we do before freezers?

For American Crust pastry:
6½ oz sunflower margarine
8 oz self-raising flour
½ tsp salt
3 tbsp cold water

In a bowl cut margarine into fairly small pieces. Add flour gradually, mixing it in with a wooden spoon. Add salt. Dribble in water, mixing quickly but thoroughly. (This pastry can be sticky, but is worth the awkwardness!) Put aside in a cool place for 1 hour, or in the 'fridge for 30 minutes.

Roll out pastry on to a floured surface, and shape into a 7″ pie dish. I often have enough left over to lattice the top after I've added the plums. Cook at 400°F (200°C), Gas Mark 6, for 35–40 minutes.

One of the most endearing qualities of trifle is its ability to improve with keeping. A number made and stored above pussy-height on the stone pantry shelves gives one a wonderfully comforting feeling as the Flower Festival advances. That shelf is always empty before the five days are over.

Festival Trifle

Serves 8

One sponge layer, i.e. half a Victoria
6 tbsp sherry
2 tbsp grape juice
4 oz strawberries
4 oz raspberries
4 oz plums, stoned and sliced
4 oz sultanas
custard
whipped or ice cream
slivered almonds
plums, quartered, to decorate

In a cut-glass bowl – it's Festival time – make up the trifle from sponge through fruit to custard: Place the sponge in the bottom of the bowl, breaking it up to fit. Soak with the sherry and grape juice. Next, mix the fruit and add to the bowl. Make up the custard – I take the easy way this month and use powder! – and allow to cool slightly. Pour over the fruit. Chill. Use either whipped or ice-cream, depending on time, for topping, and decorate with slivered almonds or a mixture of red and golden plum quarters.

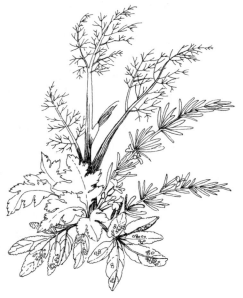

BREAD AND CAKES

One may not live on bread alone, but even at Flower Festival time one shouldn't live without it. Since calories are burnt up frenetically at this period, I bake several batches of this substantial and filling bread.

Oatey Bread

Use the normal wholemeal bread method (see January), with each 1 lb of wholemeal flour reduced to 12 oz and the remaining 4 oz being porridge oats.

Festival Buns

Makes 12 buns
4 oz butter
4 oz demerara sugar
2 eggs, beaten
4 oz self-raising flour
2 oz sultanas
¼ oz mixed orange and lemon peel
¼ oz caraway seeds
milk to mix

Cream butter and sugar. Beat in eggs. Add remainder of ingredients and mix well. Half-fill 12 bun-cases and bake for 15–20 minutes at 375°F (190°C), Gas Mark 5. Nice with Russian ice cream coffee.

While the plums have been plummeting in, out in the orchard apples (on trees grown from pips by my mother forty years ago) have been ripening. With less hurried days, I make

Apple Loaf

4 oz butter
4 oz demerara sugar
2 eggs, beaten
8 oz wholemeal flour
2 lb apples, diced
2 oz sultanas
pinch of nutmeg

Use a non-stick tin, as for bread. Cream butter and sugar in a bowl. Add beaten eggs. Fold in flour. Core and dice (I never peel) apples finely and add to the bowl with sultanas, nutmeg and remainder of flour. Spoon into tin, and bake for 1½ hours at 325°F (170°C), Gas Mark 3. Serve hot or cold with cinnamon butter.

HERBS OF THE MONTH

Egyptian, or Tree, Onion *Allium cepa var. proliferum*
Hardy perennial, to 2 ft

Recorded by Dalechamp in 1587, the title of this onion is strange, suggesting a plant of hot climates. In fact, it hails from Canada and is as hardy as a dandelion.

Sometimes regarded as a novelty, Egyptian onions deserve to be used much more widely. They are deliciously pungent (and so says one who is not overly smitten with the charms of onions in general) when chopped raw in salads; milder when cooked in soups or stews. The young leaves can be cut and used as chives. This is an all-use plant, the underground bulbs being quite tasty but tougher than the smaller stem bulbs.

Egyptian onions contain Vitamins A, B1, B2, B5, C and E, as well as nicotinamide, glucokinins, flavonoid glycosides and pectin. They are used to reduce blood pressure and blood-sugar levels. The thick, fleshy leaves produce an antiseptic juice; just tear off a piece and squeeze on to minor cuts and grazes. Also rub on the skin, as a cleansing tonic. The juice of this herb has also been recommended as a hair-promoter, though I've had no reason to test this personally! Reduce the bulbs by boiling – or crush them, if you have the gadget – to make a strongly-flavoured but effective hot drink to treat coughs, colds, bronchitis, laryngitis and gastro-enteritis.

The leaves are strong, cylindrical and early to grow in the spring. At the tips of the stems, as the season advances, grow clusters of small, purply-skinned onions. If these are not picked when young, small roots and shoots grow, until the stems becoming top-heavy, keel over. The baby roots on the growing onions quickly burrow down into the soil, and next season produce plants of their own around the parent plant. After a season or two, when the bed is well-established, surplus onions can be picked for winter use.

Skirret *Sium sisarium*
Hardy perennial, 2–4 ft

Much valued in China from earliest times as a kitchen herb, skirret's delectable root later made such an impact on the Roman world that Tiberius accepted it as a tribute. It was introduced to northern Europe in the sixteenth century and quickly became a prized root vegetable. Its obliging speed of reproduction ensured its popularity in even the poorest gardens. In 1699, John Evelyn wrote of skirret with expansive zeal: 'Exceedingly nourishing, wholesome and delicate; of all the root kind, not subject to be windy. This excellent root . . . is very acceptable to all palates.'

The tender young shoots of spring can be stir-fried, chopped finely in salads, or quickly steamed as an entree served with sour cream. The roots can be steamed or boiled, used as a vegetable in their own right; as a dressing for meat; chopped into soups, stews and pies; or diced in salads.

Culpeper, too, was generous: 'Wholesome food,' he said, of the spring shoots, 'of a cleansing nature, and easy digestion.' Then, as now, they have diuretic properties – as do the boiled roots, which have been used to treat liver complaints.

In the garden, skirret is ornamental as well as useful, and its small white flowers are long-lasting in arrangements. The seventeenth-century herbalist, John Gerard, wrote quaintly of 'Skirrets': 'The stalkes be short, the floures in the spokie tufts are white . . . this is that *Siser* or Skirret which Tiberius the Emperour commanded to bee conveied unto him from Gelduba a castle about the river of Rhene . . . a medicinable herbe, which the Emperour did so much commend, insomuch that he desired the same to be brought unto him every yeare out of Germany.'

Plant near the back of the herb border, in full sun and fairly rich soil. Grow skirret from seed or crown division, giving plants a distance of 12 in. Shoots can be cut in spring, but don't rob the plants in their first year. Lift the roots in autumn and either store in sand like carrots, or blanch and freeze. The old gardeners used to feed their skirret beds regularly with comfrey manure, to harvest the finest roots come autumn.

Angelica *Angelica archangelica*
Fairly short-lived perennial, to 8 ft

Comparatively speaking, this is a 'young' herb, with a mere five centuries of documented use. A legend from central Europe has St Michael Archangel, in a vision, extolling the herb's power to protect the grower or wearer from evil. Certainly it was used as an inhalant in times of plague. Later, with even more pleasant results, it was used in a variety of liqueurs such as Benedictine and Chartreuse. It is also said to have gained the name St Michael's Herb, because it flowered around St Michael's Day: in Britain, it's usually finished ripening its seed by that time.

Cook the fresh stems and leaves with tart fruits, as a natural sweetener (2 oz of herb to 1 lb of fruit is a fair guide). Shredded young leaves are tasty in salads. Peel the stems and midribs of older leaves and use as·celery; they also act as a breath-freshener and appetizer. The seeds, produced in abundance, can be used in cakes and pastries, reducing the need for sugar.

It has been said that the test of a good cook is to candy angelica successfully (and that's meant to be encouraging!). Cut fairly young stems into 4 in. lengths and soak in cold salted water (¼ oz to 1 ¼ pints) for 10–15 minutes, to 'fix' the colour. Rinse thoroughly, and boil in unsalted water until tender. Strip away any tough fibres, and then candy in the normal way. As well as being enjoyable 'neat', candied angelica is tasty in jams and pies.

Try angelica tea, using young fresh leaves. Stir in a dash of lemon juice, and a suggestion of honey, and you have the perfect appetite-improver. Used sparingly – and if preferred, cold – it alleviates bronchial catarrh.

And the seed quickly loses vitality, so sow it as soon as it's ripe, preferably in seedpans or trays which can be over-wintered in a cold frame. This is a relatively hardy perennial, but often dies after three or four seasons. If the seed-heads are picked off soon after flowering, its life can be extended for another season or two. In southern areas it will self-sow freely around the old crowns. The great ribbed stems, with pretty, light-green leaves looking more delicate than they really are, rise to 6 ft, sometimes 8, so this is definitely not a herb for the windowbox.

Mullein *Verbascum thapsus*
Hardy biennial, to 8 ft

This is an aristocrat among herbs, which has earned many common names including Candlewick Plant, Beggar's Blanket, Peter's Staff, Old Man's Flannel and Donkey's Ears. When Circe turned Ulysses' crew into pigs the ancient hero himself was saved by the gift of mullein, which was long-believed to have magical powers. More prosaically, the Romans used its generously felted leaves to line their sandals on wearisome route marches.

Mullein flowers are added to liqueurs, where their honey-fragrance is delicious. The flowers are non-toxic. Even the rest of the plant is only slightly toxic when used in excess or regularly over a long period. Mullein is such fun to grow, and its flowers attract so many bees which also pollinate so much else. Mullein flowers can be added to salads – they look particularly pretty with borage, chives, sweet cicely and nasturtium flowers.

The long, straight stems when lit as tapers give a soft light, kind to the eyes, for an appreciable time. Coated first with wax, their illumination is significantly prolonged. Use them for barbecues, or evening meals in the garden. Pick the flowers for *pot-pourris*, or floral arrangements. With their outer green parts removed, float the flowers in liqueurs, where they add piquancy and colour. A clear yellow dye can be made from them, as well as soothing skin tonic. Fruit such as oranges and figs can be wrapped in mullein leaves, to extend shelf-life.

Tea made from the flowers and/or the leaves can be used to alleviate bronchial, lung and chest complaints. Strain the liquid first, as the leaf-hairs may otherwise cause irritation. Oil for treating ear problems can be made from olive oil and mullein flowers: allow this to macerate for three weeks in a warm place, and strain before use. The more flowers used, the stronger the oil. A fomentation of the leaves in hot vinegar and water forms an excellent local balm for external irritations.

Mullein gets along with most soils, but needs a sunny position. Sow the seed in spring, after which self-sown seedlings will ensure continuity of supply. The plants are most ornamental, and can be freely transplanted when young. Mullein's cheerful yellow flowers open at random up the stems, from June to the frosts. No wind can fell this soldierly herb, which can be used to protect other plants, or screen unwelcome eyesores. Bees love them. CAVEAT: All parts of the plant except the flower are slightly toxic. Use with care.

September

Michaelmas daisies
September.

---

*I am come into my garden, my sister, my spouse: I
have gathered my myrrh with my spice; I have
eaten my honeycomb with my honey; I have drunk
my wine with my milk: eat, O friends; drink, yea,
drink abundantly, O beloved.*
(Song of Solomon 5:1)

September

STARTERS

Celery Salad • Soupe Coprine • Artichoke Pâté

SAVOURY LIGHT LUNCHEON/
SUPPER DISHES

---

*Sandwich Eggs • Spicy Chicken Legs
• Tomato Delight •*

DINNER (MAIN COURSE DISHES)

---

*Harvest Schnitzel • Spicy Sausage Stew
• Boeuf Jardinière •*

DESSERTS

Southern Treat • Rhubarb Cheesecake • Tansy Treat

BREAD AND CAKES

Soya Bread • Barm Cake • Blackberry Cake

HERBS OF THE MONTH

Tansy • Hop • Bistort • Santolina

Except where otherwise stated, each recipe caters for four people

---

September is a time for catching up with literary and horticultural work which has piled up during the Flower Festival. The nights draw in ever sooner, and heavier morning dews stay longer. It's also a month for hauling timber into the stable, to be sawn and stacked on winter days.

One September, I flew to Paris. The horse chestnuts in the Champs Elysèes were shedding their conkers, Eiffel's Tower creaked ominously in an early gale, and the bookstalls on the quay at Notre Dame were still a bargain-hunter's paradise. When one is abroad, it's strange how quickly one slips into the local mood: though every car on the streets seemed to have at least one dent, and every horn incapable of remaining silent for more than a few seconds, when it came to catching the plane back I found myself saying to the taxi-driver, 'Vite! Vite!' I don't remember much of the scenery, but the plane hadn't left by the time we took the last corner into Le Bourget, on two wheels.

STARTERS

The French are artist(e)s in salad-making. I've modified one I enjoyed in a little restaurant near the Opera House.

Celery Salad

6 celery sticks, blanched
½ oz French sorrel leaves
6 eggs, hard-boiled
2 bulbs Finocchio fennel
2 small lettuces
1 carrot, grated
½ lb red and yellow tomatoes, sliced
½ lb Mozzarella cheese, sliced
½ lb crispy bacon rashers, cooked
6 bistort leaves (soaked first for 2–3 hours to reduce oxalic acid content)
Vinaigrette Dressing:
6 tbsp olive oil
2 tbsp vinegar
½ tsp each parsley, chervil, thyme and tarragon, chopped

Chop celery into ½ in. pieces and soak in iced water for 30 minutes. In another bowl soak sorrel. Drain and dry. Shell and chop the eggs. Slice fennel finely. Arrange a bed of lettuce and sorrel. Mix the ingredients for the vinaigrette in a medium-sized bowl. Add remainder of ingredients into the blended vinaigrette, and lay on top of the salad bed. Yellow tomatoes are sometimes difficult to buy, if you don't grow your own, but they do brighten up a dish.

A little distance up the lane we have a regularly productive patch of Coprinus *(Ink-Cap, Shaggy Cap, Lawyer's Wig) fungi. Picked before the 'wig' curls up at its base, they make a delicious*

Soupe Coprine

Serves 8
1 ½ lb coprinus (stems and wigs)
2 oz butter
1 garlic clove, chopped
1 ½ pints chicken stock
1 tsp parsley, chopped
4–6 leaves hop
salt to taste
½ pint double cream

Wash and slice coprinus. In a deep pan melt butter and fry garlic for 2 minutes. Add coprinus and stock. Bring to boil, add parsley, hop and salt, cover and simmer for 30 minutes. Stir in cream just before serving. Make a lot of this – coprinus are in season so briefly. It freezes well.

I love them so much that I always start to rob my Jerusalem artichokes in September: I know they need a few frosts for more flavour. So my first recipe of the season is one in which the young artichokes complement the chicken deliciously.

Artichoke Pâté

Serves 8
3 oz fatty bacon
6 oz chicken, cooked
1 clove garlic, whole
6 oz pigs liver paste
8 oz artichokes
water for boiling
1 tsp each parsley, oregano and chives
salt to taste

Fry bacon and garlic quickly, and blend the fat with the liver paste. Wash, scrub and dice artichokes. Bring to boil and cook for 10 minutes. Save water for soup. Dice bacon finely. Mix with chicken. In a deep bowl, blend into liver paste. Add artichokes, herbs and seasoning. Pack into ramekins, chill and serve with freshly baked potatoes.

LIGHT SAVOURY DISHES

Eating out, either on the terrace or in the tresaunt, *is becoming more infrequent. Also, as herbaceous borders and rockeries come to a hiatus in their year, meals al fresco tend to give one mental contortions in trying to remember all the jobs virtually screaming to be done. I'm convinced weeds and dead-heads burgeon when they see the chairs and tables being carried out.*

I tend to make a decent amount of this, and any left over goes into stuffing aubergines or tomatoes as a starter for dinner.

Sandwich Eggs

8 eggs, hard-boiled
4 red tomatoes
1 cucumber (half, if it's large)
pinch of santolina (cotton lavender)
1 tsp each of oregano and dill
salt to taste

Shell and mash the eggs in a deep bowl. With a sharp knife, shred the tomatoes as fine as possible. Slice and chop cucumber. Mix, and add herbs and seasoning. Spread generously on buttered slices of malted wholemeal bread.

*It was Russia that introduced me to spices, strangely enough,
for I'd associated them with the Far East. But then, Peter the
Great's window didn't let in a devastating amount of the West.
One doesn't have to go to Asiatic Russia to feel the pull of the
Orient. It was in Moscow that I first had*

Spicy Chicken Legs

Serves 6
2 garlic cloves, chopped
olive oil
6 chicken legs
1 tsp each ground cardamom, cumin
and coriander
1 tsp black peppercorns

In a deep pan, fry garlic in oil until translucent. Add chicken legs and spices. Fry quickly until uniformly brown. Serve on a bed of hot rice, spiced and coloured with turmeric. It tastes even more colourful than it looks!

*Derbyshire's autumns don't ripen green tomatoes well, and I'm
not crazy about chutney. So to make the most of the clusters still
on the plants, I cut the fruits singly and pack in brown paper.
We're still enjoying them at Christmas. Thankfully the frosts
haven't yet arrived. There's still a fresh abundance for*

Tomato Delight

Serves 6
6 small mackerel, filleted
seasoned flour
3 tbsp olive oil
1 clove garlic, chopped
1 oz butter
2 tsp wine vinegar
3 oz mushrooms, sliced
1 lb tomatoes, chopped
1 tsp each fennel, oregano and parsley
sea salt to taste

Seal the fish in flour. In a deep pan heat 2 tbsp oil. Fry fillets, 5 minutes a side. In a second pan, heat remainder of oil and fry garlic until brown. Add butter and stir until melted. Add mushrooms and tomatoes and fry for 5–7 minutes. Stir in vinegar, and add herbs and seasoning. Lay fillets on a serving dish, and decorate with tomato mixture. I like this dish with French fried potatoes and the first of the season's parsnips.

MAIN COURSE DISHES

Indian corn (sweet corn) is like Chinese artichokes: one walks down the garden to get it, and runs back to the kitchen to cook it before the freshness wears off – in the case of Indian corn, before the sugar turns to starch.

In the days when we kept poultry, the chopped corn was called 'kibbled maize' – for all I know, it may still be so. Today, only the coldest, wettest summers spell no cobs, so we're able to enjoy this vegetable at no remove. I like it in

Harvest Schnitzel

4 cobs Indian corn (sweet corn)
3 lb pork fillets
1 tbsp seasoned flour
1 garlic clove, chopped
2½ oz sunflower margarine
2½ tbsp olive oil
For the sauce:
1 lb flat mushrooms, sliced
1 tbsp olive oil
3 oz sunflower margarine
1 tbsp wholemeal flour
8 tbsp chicken and garlic stock
8 tbsp white wine
pinch of cumin
salt to taste
1 tbsp soured cream

Scald the corn cobs and strip grains. Slice fillets into six portions. Beat flat. Coat with seasoned flour and fry with corn and garlic in margarine and oil until lightly browned.

While the meat is cooking, fry mushrooms in oil and margarine. Add flour and stock, wine and seasoning. Stir to the boil and simmer for 2–4 minutes. Stir in soured cream and pour over corn and meat. Serve with roasted potatoes and grilled courgettes.

This is a month when I eat out a lot: invitations held over during the holidays and the Flower Festival pour in. It's nice to visit friends' gardens and enjoy their cooking, before the dark evenings really close in. Living in the country largely means hibernating until British Summer Time rears its foreign but welcome head at the end of March. One of my favourite dishes, as the chillier evenings arrive, is a bit like Goulash, but quicker.

Spicy Sausage Stew

Serves 4

1 clove garlic, chopped
3 tbsp olive oil
2 tbsp paprika
1 tsp each of cumin, coriander and cardamom
1 lb flat mushrooms
salt and pepper to taste
1 lb tomatoes, quartered
1 lb potatoes, cooked and sliced
1 lb beef sausages, cooked
¼ pint soured cream

In a deep pan fry garlic in oil until brown. Stir in paprika, herbs, mushrooms, seasoning and quartered tomatoes. Bring to boil, cover and simmer for 15–20 minutes. Add potatoes and sliced sausages and simmer for 8–10 minutes. Stir in soured ceram just prior to serving. I like this dish with mashed parsley potatoes and carrot discs.

The swifts, who have swooped and shrieked across the garden since May, have left without a last goodbye. Each day more and more swallows gather broodingly on the telephone wires, little heaps of debris on the old garage floor mute reminders of the summer's frenetic activity in the exquisitely crafted nests on the rafters above.

Happily, we haven't yet had a frost, and the dahlias still are gorgeous. Each day friends depart with bootloads of colour, after feasting yet again on my September speciality. It has a grand name but all it really is, is beef roasted to a turn and a cross-section of vegetables in season.

Boeuf Jardinière

Serves 6
¼ lb each parsnips and carrots
¼ lb each salsify and scorzonera
3 lb silverside of beef
2 oz beef dripping
2 garlic cloves, chopped
2 bay leaves
½ tsp each of sage, thyme and oregano
4 peppercorns
salt to taste
beef stock
¼ lb runner beans
¼ lb sugar snap peas (mange-tout)
¼ lb asparagus peas

Prepare the vegetables, dicing the roots. In a deep pan fry the sliced beef in dripping until brown on both sides. Add garlic and brown. Add root vegetables, herbs and seasoning. Bring to boil, cover and simmer for 2½–3 hours, adding beef stock if liquid evaporates. Cook legumes in salted boiling water for 5–7 minutes. Arrange meat on hot dish and decorate with vegetables. Skim off the fat and use juices as gravy. Serve with jacket potatoes. It won't stop winter coming, but it certainly makes one feel warmer.

DESSERTS

Gardeners often go to great lengths to cultivate exotic plants which seem totally unsuited to their demesnes. Equally illogically, northern cooks now and then succumb to the temptation of Mediterranean dishes. September for me spells the simple, mouth-wateringly exotic

Southern Treat

8 fresh Italian figs
¼ pint double cream
¼ pint natural yoghurt
4 tbsp demerara sugar
pinch of cinnamon

To loosen the purple skins of these royals among figs, immerse the fruits for a minute in next-to-boiling water. Drain, peel and quarter. Beat cream into yoghurt, and spoon on to shell dishes. Add figs and sprinkle with sugar. Chill, and dust with cinnamon on serving.

We spend a couple of afternoons on a friend's estate picking hazel nuts for the winter. Some of the ripest I use with the last fresh rhubarb of the season for

Rhubarb Cheesecake

3 oz sunflower margarine
3 oz demerara sugar
16 digestive biscuits, crumbled
12 lemon balm leaves
The filling:
2 eggs
1 ½ lb soft curd cheese
¼ pint double cream
6 oz demerara sugar
1 ½ lb rhubarb, chopped and cooked
pinch of nutmeg
2 drops almond essence
hazel nuts to garnish

Cream margarine and sugar. Crush biscuits with a rolling pin in a polythene bag. Blend in creamed sugar. Lay balm leaves on flan dish and press biscuit base well in. Cook at 350°F (180°C), Gas Mark 4, for 10 minutes.

Beat eggs into cheese and cream. Add sugar and fruit, nutmeg and essence. Spoon on to biscuit base and continue baking at 350°F (180°C), Gas Mark 4, for 30 minutes. Decorate with chopped hazel nuts before serving hot or cold.

When I began to grow tansy the plants used to be smothered in aphids by the autumn. But for some reason after that first year the aphids departed and have not yet returned – so we can enjoy lots of

Tansy Treat

It's not really a recipe: just a few tansy leaves chopped fine and blended into a custard, with a pinch of nutmeg or cinnamon, and 4 oz of ground almonds.

Michaelmas (29 September) brings its pink and purple drifts of Michaelmas daisies. As I work near these, harvesting barley, butterflies are making the most of a sunny afternoon: small tortoiseshells, painted ladies, peacocks, red admirals. Soon they will be papery dark shadows high up in the ceiling corners of the upper landing – until next year.

BREAD AND CAKES

Once difficult to obtain, soya flour is now in many health food shops. It's choc-ful of protein.

Soya Bread

I use my usual wholemeal bread recipe (see January), with 3 tbsp soya to each 1 lb of wholemeal flour – and only a thin film of butter on each slice when serving.

*My grandmother used to make a Yorkshire Barm Cake. Mine
is quite different, but one we've enjoyed now for many years.*

Barm Cake

4 oz butter
6 oz demerara sugar
2 eggs
½ oz fresh barm (yeast)
¼ pint warm water
½ tsp bicarbonate of soda
½ lb strong plain flour
¾ pound sultanas
2 oz ground almonds
pinch of allspice
salt to taste
slivered almonds to decorate

Use a 7 in. non-stick cake tin. Cream butter
and sugar. Beat in eggs. Melt barm in water and
add, with bicarbonate of soda. Fold in flour,
fruit and almonds. Add spice and seasoning.
Bake at 350°F (180°C), Gas Mark 4, for
1½–1¾ hours. Decorate with slivered
almonds.

The hips of Rosa moyesii *'Geranium' are ready for harvesting; a fiddly business, but fragrant and so worthwhile. Some boxes of hips are set aside for Harvest Festival. Most find their way into syrup jars, and some of the rest into this cake. It combines two lovely fruits, and is nice to freeze for Christmas tea-parties.*

Blackberry Cake

4 oz butter
4 oz caster sugar
8 oz plain flour
2 eggs, beaten
rosehip syrup to mix
blackberries for decoration

Use a non-stick 7 in. tin. Cream butter and sugar. Add flour and beaten eggs. Mix to a soft consistency with rosehip syrup, and bake for 1 hour at 350°F (180°C), Gas Mark 4. Be generous with the blackberry decoration.

Meld some extra blackberries and a dash of rosehip syrup into the ice cream you serve with this fragrant cake.

Many annual herbs need their seed carefully harvesting in September – herbs like coriander, dill, rocket, nasturtium and basil. Others, like garlic, lavender, mint and thyme, need dividing and/or layering, and new beds laid out. We're only a whisker away from autumn now. Next month the swallows will have gone, but St Luke might let us have another 'Little Summer'.

HERBS OF THE MONTH

Tansy *Tanacetum vulgare,* (Syn. *Chrysanthemum vulgare*)
Perennial, to 2 ft

Tanacetum is thought to come from the Greek *athanaton*, 'undying', and a sprig of it used to be placed as a symbol of immortality in coffins. It was also used in embalming. Tansy is one of the herbs dedicated to Our Lady. It was grown in the physic garden at the monastery of St Gall in Switzerland, over 1,000 years ago. The garden was Charlemagne's favourite, and he had its design replicated on all his imperial estates.

Bygone Easters used to see Tansy, as a rich custardy pudding, on the festive tables. Rub the fresh leaves on meat, for a rosemary-like flavour. They can also be stewed with rhubarb, and used to flavour sausages, meat pies, stuffings and omelettes. The flowers give a gentle yellow tint when added to flour, as well as giving it a nice tangy flavour (add 1 dessertsp flowers to 1 lb of flour).

More prosaically, tansy was used as a strewing herb, with insecticidal and disinfectant properties. Today we grow it near fruit trees to repel insects, hang bunches indoors to deter flies, strew dried sprigs under carpets, and wrap meat in its leaves as a preservative. The yellow pincushion flowers dry well for 'everlastings', and can also be boiled for a yellow-green woollen dye.

Used sparingly as a flower/leaf wash, tansy relieves rheumatism, bruises and sprains. Test with a very weak solution first, as some skins are allergic to it.

Surplus leaves added to the compost heap bolster its potassium content.

Hop *Humulus lupulus*
Climber, to 20 ft

Introduced to French and German gardens in the ninth century, hop bines had already been grown for long by the Romans. In Britain two bitter herbs, costmary and ground ivy, held sway until as late as the sixteenth century hops were introduced. From the herb's fondness for twining its bines (stems) around willows, Pliny had called it *Lupus salictarius* ('Willow Wolf'), but extolled its virtues as a garden climber and vegetable.

The papery buds are edible, but need blanching first to remove the bitterness of lupulin. In the seventeenth and eighteenth centuries hop was an important kitchen herb, though John Evelyn writing in 1670 was less than enthusiastic, saying it 'preserve the drink indeed, but repay the pleasure in tormenting diseases and a shorter life'. Eat young shoots and the small male flowers in salads. Blanch the leaves and use in soups. The shoots can be steamed and eaten like asparagus. Make Hop Bitters with equal parts hop flowers, holy thistle and angelica stems.

The female flowers, like little dangling cones, are still used in the brewing of beers. Male flowers are much smaller, and produced on separate plants. Hops used in beer-making extend the shelf-life of the brew.

Medicinally, dried hop flowers have an efficient life of three months, after which they deteriorate quickly. They contain a natural antiseptic, and can be applied externally to ulcers; formerly they were used to treat prostate disorders. Tea made from an infusion of the flowers acts like a tonic, aids digestion and is an internal antiseptic. Hop blends well with other herbs in tea mixtures, including valerian, chamomile, balm and nepeta (add a dash of honey if you like). This herb should not be taken internally by those suffering already from depression.

Pillows stuffed with dried hop flowers aid sleep – particularly when the herb is sprinkled with alcohol. A brown dye can be obtained by boiling the leaves. Hop oil is used today in the manufacture of certain perfumes. The resilient bines can be used in basketry and a variety of wickerwork. In days of yore they were used in the manufacture of paper and cloth. The flowers are good for arrangements and *pot-pourris*. Infused, add to the water for a relaxing bath.

Grow hops from seed or division, spacing the plants 3 ft apart. Flowers are usually produced in the third season from seed. Cut the bines back to ground-level in the autumn. Hops make pretty pot plants, but rarely flower indoors.

Give this herb a position in full sun, with a wall or trellis up which to climb. It is a lovely plant for the patio, needing no tying. If you live in an 'olde worlde' house, ceiling beams decorated with hops at the end of the season look beautiful through the short days of winter.

Bistort *Polygonum bistorta,* 'Snakeweed'
Hardy perennial, to 3 ft

'Bistorta' (twice-twisted) refers to the strangely contorted rhizome or swollen underground stem. Of the 200 or so species in the genus *polygonum*, it was not until the Renaissance that bistort was accepted into the pharmacopoeias. Today Swiss, French and Russian medical practices still use this herb.

From earliest times the food value of bistort has been recognized. Today the wheel has turned full circle, and this herb is being grown in many new gardens. It contains Vitamin C as well as oxalic and tannic acid. To reduce the oxalic acid, soak the roots well before roasting and serving like parsnips. Tear the young leaves into salads. The young shoots and leaves can be steamed or boiled as spinach. A north-country traditional dish is Easter Ledges – a pudding served at Easter and made largely with young bistort leaves. Use this herb, too, with nettles, parsley and sweet cicely for an iron-rich spring soup.

A recipe which is good to eat with bacon or veal is a variation on the old Magiants Pudding, itself similar to Easter Ledges: pick a handful each of young leaves of dandelion, bistort and nettle; steep them in boiling water for 15 minutes. Drain, and chop the leaves fairly finely. Mix in 1 oz boiled barley, 1 chopped hard-boiled egg and ½ oz butter or sunflower margarine. Season with sea salt and a little coriander, and stir well. Bake in a pudding basin for

5–10 minutes and serve hot or cold.

Formerly, bistort was used to treat tubercular patients. Today, dry the roots and pulverize; infuse as a tea for diarrhoea, and – dry – to staunch bleeding from wounds. A decoction of the root is an effective mouthwash for ulcers, and as a gargle helps fight coughs, colds and sore throats. A brew made from young bistort leaves, nettle tops and dandelion leaves, used to be drunk as a tonic by country children. It is used also in veterinary medicine. In addition, the root has been used to tan leather.

The pink flowers of bistort are attractive and long-lasting in arrangements. If left on the plants they provide colour from midsummer to the frosts. Give this herb sun or shade, but definitely moist soil. Division of the creeping rootstock can be in the spring or autumn. Divide regularly, or this herb will spread far and wide.

Santolina *Santolina chamaecyparissus* (Syn. *C. incana*) 'Cotton Lavender' Fairly tender evergreen, to 18 in.

Known for centuries in its native Mediterranean climes, santolina is neither a lavender nor cotton, but one of the numerous daisy clan. Britain is indebted to French Huguenot garden designers for introducing this tidy knot-garden favourite – though north of a line from Teeside to the Dee, a cold damp winter can kill this herb. As its name suggests, it's virtually a little tree: in fact, the Romans called it *habrotanum*, and the Greeks *abrotonon*.

It was among the herbs taken out by the Pilgrim Fathers to America.

I love to add a pinch of santolina to Chinese artichokes (Crosnes) just before serving. Try this herb also in soups (especially mushroom) and stews – but sparingly, for it's an acquired taste. A reviving drink for winter evenings is hot, pure orange juice with a wee sprig of santolina.

Culpeper considered this herb 'an antidote for all sorts of poisons'. Santolina tea used to be taken as a kidney tonic, and to treat jaundice. Today an infusion of 1 oz leaves to 1 pint boiling water is still a remedy for worms, and is also taken to regulate menstruation.

The yellow button flowers dry well for *pot-pourris*. Santolina is one of the most effective insect-repellents. Dry it and stuff into sachets for wardrobes, bookshelves, kitchen and pantry cupboards, and under cushions and carpets.

The silvery foliage is attractive all the year round, and the flowers appear from mid to late summer. This herb likes to grow in the crevices of a wall or rockery, in full sun. Never site it where falling autumn leaves can lodge on the foliage and rot it. Stem cuttings taken in late spring root quickly and easily. To keep the bushes tidy, clip to shape as soon as the flowers fade. Keep santolina well away from rue: both are credited with discouraging the toxicity of poisons, but are not compatible with each other in the garden.

October

the vine –
in the tomato house.
October

Thou visitest the earth, and waterest it: thou
greatly enrichest it with the river of God . . . Thou
crownest the year with Thy goodness . . . The
pastures are clothed with flocks; the valleys also
are covered over with corn . . .
(Psalm 65:9, 11, 13)

October

STARTERS

Borshch Britaine • Salade Cardoon • Seafood Pâté

SAVOURY LIGHT LUNCHEON/
SUPPER DISHES

Mushie Toasties • Ham and Sorrel Salad
• Rectory Hot-Pot •

DINNER (MAIN COURSE DISHES)

Russian Ragout • Winter Ratatouille
• Savory Pheasant •

DESSERTS

Apple Mint Crumble • Grape Custard
• Hamburgh Jelly •

BREAD AND CAKES

Mealy Bread • Apple Tarts • Minty Date Cookies

HERBS OF THE MONTH

Pennyroyal • Winter Savory • French Marjoram
• Buckler-leaved Sorrel •

Except where otherwise stated, each recipe caters for four people

---

Way back in the forties friends from Yorkshire gave us some cuttings from their vinery: two 'Black Hamburgh' and a third from an unnamed, seedless green grape. One of the 'Black Hamburgh' cuttings took, and is trained over the conservatory roof, while a daughter-cutting is espaliered on the north-west wall of the tomato house. A year or two ago I was given a green cutting (unnamed), which is also in the tomato house, and hopefully will fruit next season.

There's one drawback about arranging grapes at Harvest Festivals. Unless one fiddles around with test-tubes, it's impossible to keep the foliage fresh. Damp moss never seems to give the soft leaves enough sustenance.

STARTERS

I dearly love Russian food but beetroot doesn't love me, so I had to watch friends enjoying Borshch on its home ground. However – Ukrainians, please forgive me – I've modified your speciality into

Borshch Britaine

Serves 6
1 lb white cabbage heart
3 leeks
2 carrots
2 salsifies
1 potato
¼ lb tomatoes
2 pints chicken stock
2 cloves garlic, chopped but not fried
1 bay leaf
1 tsp each coriander and cumin
1 tbsp parsley
1 tsp French marjoram
1 tsp soft brown sugar
salt to taste
5 fl. oz soured cream

Wash and drain cabbage, putting 4 oz leaves to one side and finely shredding the rest. Wash, trim and shred leeks, carrots, salsifies and potatoes. Purée tomatoes.

Into a deep pan pour stock, vegetables, garlic, herbs, sugar and seasoning. Bring to boil, cover and simmer for 1 hour. 15 minutes prior to serving, shred remaining cabbage and add to borshch, thinning if necessary with more stock. Fold in the soured cream just before serving with fried croûtons and a garnish of finely-sliced courgettes.

After the television screening of Harry Dodson's Victorian
Kitchen Garden – *which made me long for a video to see it again*
and again – friends met me at church and in town with: 'You
had those big thistle things at Harvest last year!' My cardoons
had looked very statuesque at the west end.

Since the plants are too large to earth up like celery, we use
plaited rushes from the pond as a thatch. In a few weeks' time
the great ribbed stems, prickly for unwary fingers, are ready for

Salade Cardoon

Serves 6
6 cardoon midribs, blanched
a little olive oil
12 yellow tomatoes
3 lettuces
bunch of landcress
3 roots winter radish (mooli)
4 medium courgettes
small bunch black grapes
4 small celery sticks
¼ lb French beans
¼ lb peas
1 clove garlic, chopped
few leaves each of lemon balm,
tarragon, bergamot, pennyroyal and
winter savory

Only the cardoons need to be cooked. Wash
and slice the stems. Fry quickly in a little olive
oil until golden brown. Allow to cool, and
then incorporate with the prepared salad.

Derbyshire's rich in history but at school local history didn't play much of a part, until we were studying the period of the Babington Plot. On the following Saturday afternoon, to gain extra material for my essay, we went over to Chesterfield to visit the quaint little cottage – once the Cock & Pynot Inn – where the plotters met. It's now simply called The Revolution House.

The rain came down in stair-rods, so we had to eat our picnic in the old 1940 Rover '12', which years later I was to learn to drive. I've always associated seafood pâté with the Revolution House, since we joked that the sea couldn't have been wetter than Derbyshire that day. This is based on an old Yorkshire recipe of my grandmother's.

Seafood Pâté

fish stock
½ lb cod fillets
pinch of nutmeg
milled parsley
butter
¾ lb prawns, cooked
¾ lb, shrimps, cooked

Using just enough stock to cover cod, simmer fillets in a pan for 10–15 minutes. Reduce stock to 1 tbsp. Flake the cod and season. Allow to cool. Weigh the mix, and equal it with butter. Add prawns and shrimps and simmer in a pan for 3–5 minutes. Press into pottery dishes or ramekins. Cool, and seal with clarified butter (butter purified by melting and filtering). Serve chilled.

LIGHT SAVOURY DISHES

It's a bad year for the mushrooms when we get early frosts – but then, fungi are unpredictable. I spent some years in mycological research and found fungi a bit like the weather: the more technology probes into the subject, the more incomprehensible it seems. Gem, one of my St Bernard dogs, used to race me to the mushrooms in the high fields. Emma, my present Saint, has no liking for them.

While frosts hold off, our luncheon and supper guests will continue to enjoy this light dish. One day, I'll give it a more sophisticated title.

Mushie Toasties

All I do, is grill a couple of pounds of mushrooms, rolling them afterwards in a glorious mixture of crumbled marjoram and basil. Serve on hot buttered rounds of Mealy Bread (see p.168). Marjoram and field mushrooms go well together, but marjoram's too strong to use with *Coprinus* (see September).

Usually I soak French buckler-leaved sorrel before working it into a dish; but in this recipe the oxalic acid, I find, offsets the saltiness of the ham. Still, if you react badly to it, soak the sorrel first.

Ham and Sorrel Salad

Serves 6
1 clove garlic, halved
3 endive
1 lb smoked ham, thinly sliced
6 eggs, hard-boiled
1 lb petits pois
small bunch of sorrel
salt to taste

Halve the garlic clove and rub around the inside of the salad bowl. On a bed of endive (I like my endive unblanched – but I haven't a sweet tooth) arrange rolls of ham, thin slices of egg, and peas and sorrel in confusion. This salad is nice served with horseradish relish and hot, unbuttered wholemeal rolls.

Sunday is supposed to be a day of rest – but preaching and taking services usually means meals here on a Sunday are the quickest and lightest of the week. Rarely do we have time for dinner, so this next dish has evolved, to keep us going in between commitments. Many a sermon's not only been prepared, but delivered, on Rectory Hot-Pot nourishment. And it's not only enjoyed on Sundays.

Rectory Hot-Pot

Oh, how the purists will hold up their hands in horror! As I've said earlier, my stock-pot is always in use. During the week – with Sunday in mind – chicken legs, bits of liver, beef and vegetables of all kinds find their way into this deliciously fragrant potion. And all one needs to do, come busy Sundays, is to boil it up, simmer for a few minutes, and dig in the serving spoon.

MAIN COURSE DISHES

Leaves, leaves and more leaves. Our long gravelled drive and miles of garden paths attract them like peanuts attract the squirrels. Sack upon sack of nutritious beech leaves go on to the compost heaps, and hours each day, weather permitting, are spent in this seasonal but not desperately exciting job.

Still, even now, tiny grey-green spears here and there tell of the promise of snowdrops come January – and every morning more seed catalogues with improbably colourful illustrations are left in the post-box. From the time I helped my father plan the new season's vegetables, I've loved seed catalogues. And this winter's orders will surely follow the custom of being larger than the last.

Here is a warming stew, really mostly of leftovers, for evenings that are getting colder as well as longer.

Russian Ragout

Serves 6–8
2 lb parsnips, slivered
2 garlic cloves, chopped
1 lb beef, chopped and cooked
1 lb beef sausage, chopped and cooked
1 lb lean bacon, chopped and cooked
1 tsp each of pennyroyal and winter savory
4 oz Cheshire cheese, grated
salt to taste
beef stock
parsley garnish

Bring parsnips and garlic to the boil, and simmer for 10 minutes in a covered pan. In a deep casserole layer ingredients, topping off with the cheese. Season, and almost cover with stock. Cook for 15 minutes at 350°F (180°C), Gas Mark 4, adding stock if necessary. Garnish with parsley on serving.

*We usually get our first snow flurries in October. I remember
one year when a nearby farmer's caravan field looked like an
Eskimo village for a couple of unseasonal October days. It puts
one in mind of July Ratatouille, and so of the short-day variety:*

Winter Ratatouille

Serves 6–8
½ lb salsify
½ lb scorzonera
½ lb parsnips, or parsnips and carrots mixed
¼ lb cabbage, shredded
¼ lb cauliflower curds
¼ lb Brussels sprouts
1 clove garlic
¼ lb crosnes (Chinese artichokes)
olive oil
pinch each of winter savory and hyssop
salt to taste
½ lb tomatoes

Wash and prepare vegetables. Leave tomatoes aside. In a deep pan heat the oil and add ingredients and seasoning. Cover and simmer for 35–40 minutes, stirring to mix well. Serve hot, with garnish of raw tomatoes, and fried croûtons.

*A local farmer, some years ago, reared some nice batches of
pheasants in his incubator. Pheasant eggs need 28 days to hatch,
so a domestic hen's no use as a sitter, getting restless when her
21 days are up. Now my Jerusalem artichokes – pheasants'
favourite winter delight – are under attack. But something of
a truce is called, since occasionally we enjoy*

Savory Pheasant

2 pheasants, hung and dressed
1 garlic clove
4 tbsp winter savory
water or stock to boil
salt to taste

So simple: boil as for a normal chicken, topping up the stock as evaporation occurs, and allowing 35 minutes per 1 lb of bird. Delicious with jacket potatoes and carrots.

DESSERTS

Scrumping is a way of daily life now. It's also a battle between me and the wasps. But it's a good harvest. I climb up the trees to secure the best apples for the Harvest Festival. The 'dimmocky' ones are rendered down in great pans of nutmeg-dusted water – boiled into a mushy fortune for the freezer. I never, never peel our apples: all they get is quartering and coring. Some, I can't wait to make into

Apple Mint Crumble

Serves 4, generously
6 lemon-scented geranium leaves
1 ½ lb apples, cored and quartered
1 oz soft brown sugar
For the crumble:
6 oz wholemeal flour
3 oz butter
2 ½ oz soft brown sugar

Into a 3 pint pie dish shred the geranium leaves. Top with sugared apples. Sift flour into a mixing bowl and rub in butter. Dust in sugar. Spoon the mixture on to the fruit, pressing down gently. Bake on a tray in the centre of the oven for 40–45 minutes at 400°F (200°C), Gas Mark 6. Serve with mint ice cream.

Here's a quick dessert which is quintessentially October.

Grape Custard

Simply an ordinary custard (give it a pinch of nutmeg and cinnamon), with ¼ lb de-seeded grapes per diner stirred in, 3 minutes before serving.

This next dessert is equally easy – but after all, with so many grapes a-begging . . .

Hamburgh Jelly

I like to use lemon jelly, but suit yourself. De-seed grapes and add as many as you can spare(!) when the jelly is half-set. Decorate on serving with more grapes (de-seeded – it's annoying both to crunch the seeds or to extract them at table).

BREAD AND CAKES

We've never had so many flours to choose from. Bread-making buffs (and guests) need never serve the same two days running. Mealy Bread is grand with Mushie Toasties (see p.163), and much else.

Mealy Bread

In America they have a traditional Corn Bread, which is inordinately pernickety to make. I plump for a half-and-half mix of cornflour and wholewheat flour. Corn flour on its own has so little gluten one has to appeal to the dough to rise. The method is as for my usual wholemeal bread (see January). I won't spoil your anticipation, but merely say you'll love the distinctive flavour of this bread.

I'll tell you a secret: When you scrump, or pick apples straight off your own trees, it doesn't matter a toss whether they're cookers or eaters. We have both, and I make no distinction when cooking or eating them raw. Don't ask me to explain – it's probably a combination of freshness and my liking for food that tastes. I use more of the scrumpings for

Apple Tarts

Makes 16
1 lb apples, after coring
water to cook
4 oz demerara sugar
8 oz wholemeal flour
1 tsp bicarbonate of soda
1 tsp pennyroyal, chopped
salt to taste
4 oz butter
1 egg

Cook apples in a little water, with a suggestion of sugar, over a low heat until 'fallen'. Into a mixing bowl sift flour, soda, pennyroyal and salt. Rub in fat to a crumbly texture. Fold in sugar and beaten egg. Knead on a floured board and roll out ⅛ in. thick. Cut 16 tops and set aside. Cut 16 bottoms and line patty-pans. Spoon fruit into dough and seal with tops. Cut ventilation slit in each tart. Bake for 15–20 minutes at 400°F (200°C), Gas Mark 6. Cool on a wire tray – or eat hot, but expect the hot tart to fall about like apple crumble!

For All Hallows, I make trays of these cookies and none of them sees November.

Minty Date Cookies

¼ lb wholemeal flour
2 tsp baking powder
½ lb porridge oats
½ lb soft brown sugar
salt to taste
½ lb butter
1 egg, beaten
2 tsp mint, finely chopped
For the filling:
8 oz dates, stoned and chopped
½ cup demerara sugar
½ cup water

Mix flour, baking powder, oats, sugar and seasoning. Add in butter and beaten egg with mint. Knead lightly, and roll out ½ in. thick. Cut into 2½ in. rounds as for tarts.

Stir filling ingredients in saucepan over gentle heat until 'set'. Cool slightly. Put a spoonful between two rounds of dough and crimp edges together. Cook on a baking tray for 35–40 minutes at 350°F (180°C), Gas Mark 4. Serve hot or cold.

I suppose it's having so much woodland to the west, but October is one of the busiest months in the garden. The swallows have gone, the clocks have altered, and soon the fieldfares will be here. Already the ivy-covered walls in the orchard are busy with wrens deciding on the cosiest winter roosting-places. For winter is coming, although the dahlias still are beautiful.

HERBS OF THE MONTH

Pennyroyal *Mentha pulegium*
Hardy perennial, upright (10 in.) and
creeping (4 in.) forms

Once the king among mints, it is thought
pulegium (from *pulex*, 'flea') originated
with Pliny. Certainly in his day the smoke
from the burning leaves was used as a
fumigator. The Pilgrim Fathers included
pennyroyal in the collection of herbs they
took to the New World. By this time the
mint had a new name with French
associations: the botanist Linnaeus had
likened it to thyme (*puliol* is Old French
for 'thyme'); and its widespread use earned
it the name 'Royal Thyme', pennyroyal
was but a step from *Puliol royale*.

The dried leaves were once used to
flavour puddings. Today they are added
(sparingly) to soups, stews and stuffings. In
a weak solution, pennyroyal makes a
pleasant tea (Organy Tea).

Acting as a rubefacient, pennyroyal
leaves can be applied externally to insect
bites and skin irritations. This herb has also
been used to treat headaches, laryngitis,
nausea, nervous complaints, and as a
blood-purifier. Taken with other herbs, it
helps keep colds at bay. The constituent
pulegone (80–90 per cent of the volatile
oil) in concentrated form is toxic,
promoting abortion and capable of causing
irreversible damage to the kidneys.

The eighteenth century saw pennyroyal
valued in commerce for the menthol in its
essential oil; but primarily our forefathers
saw this herb as a water-purifier. On long
sea voyages, in particular, it was used in
the large casks of drinking water. The
herbalist Nicholas Culpeper wrote: 'Put
into unwholesome waters . . . that men
must drink, it makes them the less hurtful.'

Dry the leaves for a long-lasting
fragrance in *pot-pourris* and sachets. As in
Pliny's day, the leaves burned in incense-
burners, or dried and strewn in drawers,
on shelves, between sheets or under
carpets deter fleas and other nasties. Hang
a bunch of fresh leaves in the hall.

Given a partially shady, fairly damp
situation, the creeping pennyroyal makes
good groundcover. Plant pieces between
crazy paving, in pots on the patio, or along
the paths in the herb garden where its
pungent leaves can be bruised in passing.
Hard winters may kill it, so pot up some
roots each autumn and over-winter under
glass. Stem cuttings taken in summer will
root in water on the kitchen windowsill.
Avoid using this herb when pregnant, or
suffering from kidney complaints; and in
some cases it can cause minor skin
irritation.

Winter Savory *Satureia montana*
Rather tender evergreen bush, to 15 in.

In Roman times winter savory was a
favourite ingredient in sauces and vinegars,
its strong pungency masking any scents of
ageing in meat and adding zip to vegetables
such as peas and beans. Gardeners in
Tudor times valued it for outlining the
intricate beds of knot gardens.

It is an important constituent of salami. Use it sparingly when fresh, more liberally in the dried state, for its unique peppery flavour, with poultry, eggs and fish. Sprinkle finely chopped leaves onto soups just prior to serving. It's an all-in-one condiment, ideal for those on salt-free diets.

Crush savory leaves and apply them to wasp and bee stings, having first extracted the sting in the case of a bee. Savory tea, made from fresh or dried leaves, is a good stomach tonic and stimulant – the latter quality probably accounting for its historical use as an aphrodisiac: use 1 oz of the herb to 1 pint boiling water. Sufferers from asthma and kindred ills can find relief from this tea. Drink it also to ease the misery of PMT.

For that birthday gift which has so far eluded you, make up a sachet of dried savory leaves (or, if time presses, just use some dried sprigs, unsewn); insert between the paper and envelopes in a box of notelets or note-paper. Close the box as tightly as possible, and leave for at least two weeks for the beautiful scent to impregnate the paper.

From early days, savory has been grown near hives, to provide rich nectar for the bees. Its disinfectant properties can be used to purify a room, if the herb is burned on an open fire or in an incense-burner.

Poor, limey soil and a sunny position suit winter savory. Propagate either from spring-sown seed, or layer the shoots by pegging them into the soil and severing from the parent plant when rooting has been effected. Seeds can take up to a month to germinate. Originating from southern Europe, winter savory in Britain will appreciate winter protection. Regular clipping throughout the growing season stops the plants becoming woody, and gives a succession of tasty young shoots.

French or Pot Marjoram
Origanum onites
Hardy perennial, to 2 ft

This herb was valued in early Egyptian times medicinally and as a disinfectant and preservative. The ancient Greeks used marjoram oil as a massage after bathing. Pliny knew it as *Onitin*, in the first century. Later plantsmen and herbalists have often confused it with unrelated plants of similar flavour. French marjoram was introduced to Britain as late as the eighteenth century. More often seen than the species nowadays is the 'Compact pink-flowered' form, with dark-pink valerian-like flowers but similar properties.

Use the fresh leaves sparingly in milk dishes, allowing the leaves to steep in the milk for at least 30 minutes prior to cooking. In earlier days, when thunder threatened, dairymaids would strew marjoram around pails of new milk believing that the herb would prevent the milk souring.

Marjoram finds its true *raison d'être* in fish dishes: 'It can turn cod into turbot', my mother used to say. But since this is the strongest of all the origanums, use with a fairly niggardly hand. Sprinkle it on grilled courgettes and tomatoes. Cook whole leaves with brassicas and legumes. Use the dried or chopped leaves as parsley on new potatoes – also in soups, stews and casseroles. Sprinkle some of the pretty pink-to-mauve flowers in salads.

French marjoram induces perspiration, hence its popularity as a tea to alleviate colds, bronchitis and flu. Use it also to aid sleep and as a settler for *mal de mer*. Make an antiseptic poultice of the flowers to treat stiff necks, swollen glands and rheumaticky joints. Infuse the leaves and add to bathwater to relax tired muscles. The fresh leaves infused as a rinse condition all types and colours of hair.

Use the dried leaves and flowers in *pot-pourris* and herb pillows.

Despite its southern European origin, French marjoram rarely dies down completely, so is useful as a point of interest in the winter herb garden. Give it humus-rich soil, in full sun. The attractive pink flowers last well in arrangements, and in a warm room release a lovely aroma. Outdoors, they are eagerly sought by butterflies and bees. Dry them for winter use. There are gold and gold-tipped forms, which are less rampant than the true *O. onites*.

French Buckler-Leaved Sorrel

Rumex scutatus
Hardy perennial, to 12 in.

This, the best-flavoured and most popular of the sorrels, is native to Europe and Asia. Its sharpness was for centuries appreciated on the Continent, but is now finding increasing favour with British appetites.

The brittle, silvery-green leaves have a delicious acid, lemony taste, each leaf holding a surprising amount of juice. It blends well with cabbage and other brassicas, fresh green salads, and all egg dishes. It also acts as a meat tenderizer.

When holidaying in France, be a model guest and sample the sorrel soup with relish. At home, combine sorrel with watercress or landcress, and serve this delicious green soup cold on summery days, piping hot when the winter's upon us. Save some sorrel to use instead of apples in a tangy sauce with meat.

However, as with many herbs, moderation is the keynote: the leaves of French sorrel are a valuable source of Vitamin C, and good blood-purifiers into the bargain; but they also contain oxalic acid, which can be harmful if taken in excess. For this reason, sufferers of asthma, kidney and bladder complaints, rheumatism or gout should avoid it.

When sorrel is cooked as a vegetable in its own right, change the water once, to reduce the percentage of oxalic acid. On the plus side, use the squeezed juice from fresh leaves to remove stains from silver, and rust marks from linen.

Once established, the determined branched roots send up a succession of young plants around the parent, so that after a few seasons when the mature plants become woody and die, the new stock can be transplanted. A fresh site with new soil will extend their life by at least a year. Pinch out the flowers, which appear in June, to keep the plants growing vigorously. A rich, moist soil, not too much sun, and little or no lime suits this valuable herb. Seed can be sown *in situ* in late spring, or increase stock by root division, again in spring.

November

Stuffed Cabbage.
November

The eyes of all wait upon thee; and thou givest them
their meat in due season.
(Psalm 145:15)

November

STARTERS

Soupe Endive • Chinese Dip • Creamed Sprouts

SAVOURY LIGHT LUNCHEON/ SUPPER DISHES

*Parsnip Warmer • Roly-Poly Sausage
• Stuffed Cabbage •*

DINNER (MAIN COURSE DISHES)

*Short-Day Stew • Stuffed Potatoes
• Steak and Kidney Warmer •*

DESSERTS

*Washington Wish • Bread and Butter Pudding
• Gooseberry Tart •*

BREAD AND CAKES

Celery Loaf • Hyssop Parkin • Nutty Crunch

HERBS OF THE MONTH

Comfrey • Horehound • Feverfew • Hyssop

Except where otherwise stated, each recipe caters for four people

We don't get much fog here – in November or at any other time – but winter comes early. While the TV screen shows London trees still in leaf at the Remembrance Day cenotaph service, ours have long since fallen and are on the compost heaps.

STARTERS

A Belgian friend introduced me to endive many years ago. He grew it in long crinkly rows, lovely to see – and, like us, never blanched it. As winter draws in, it makes a delicious tangy soup.

Soupe Endive

Serves 6
2 fistfuls endive
¼ lb parsnips
¼ lb swedes
¼ lb potatoes
1 garlic clove, chopped
1 ½ oz butter
2 pints chicken stock
pinch of hyssop
sea salt
3 tbsp double cream

Wash and shred endive. Scrub and dice root vegetables. In a deep pan, fry garlic in butter until translucent. Add stock, seasoning and vegetables. Bring to boil, cover and simmer for 10–15 minutes. Crush vegetables gently with a fork to test for softness. Just before serving add the cream and heat through. Serve with fresh wholemeal rolls.

*This next starter never had a beginning, and its end is probably
a long way off since I vary the ingredients every time. It's just
one of those 'fun' dishes which grows according to season and
availability. I save time by making a lot and freezing some.*

Chinese Dip

6 oz mung bean sprouts
2 oz Parmesan cheese, grated
4 oz sultanas
4 oz nuts, chopped
pinch of ground ginger
1 clove garlic, crushed
pinch of horehound, chopped
cumin to garnish
1 lb natural yoghurt

In a large mixing bowl, blend ingredients into
the yoghurt until evenly mixed. Spoon into
individual shells for immediate use, and freeze
remainder. Garnish with a little ground cumin.

*My father grew better Brussels sprouts that I've ever managed.
He never needed to stake them, either. Perhaps the newer
varieties . . . Never mind, I keep trying. In good years, there are
enough for a few dishes of*

Creamed Sprouts

Nothing elaborate about this. Just slice 1 lb of
button sprouts as thinly as possible. Steam in
the top of a double steamer for no more than 5
minutes, transfer to a pan of double cream and
heat through. Garnish with mint. *Not* for every
day, but my sprouts are few and precious.

LIGHT SAVOURY DISHES

Bonfires – unless one's absolutely bereft of potash in the soil – aren't necessary for gardening and can, if large enough, render an otherwise useful patch of ground unproductive for a season. Far better to compost the season's haulms and leaves.

But I don't object to enjoying bonfire recipes indoors! Parsnips, for instance, have now been frosted and are better dug ahead of the severe weather, and before canker attacks the crowns. Years ago we baked them in the bonfire embers, with potatoes. There's far less waste with

Parsnip Warmer

Serves 4
2 lb fillet steak
olive oil
fresh wholemeal breadcrumbs
2 lb parsnips
water to boil
2 oz sunflower margarine
salt to taste
1 tsp horehound, chopped
1 egg

Slice meat into fairly thick pieces. Coat with oil and dust with breadcrumbs. Roast in a shallow tin at 425°F (220°C), Gas Mark 7, for 45–60 minutes.

Wash, scrub and slice parsnips. Season and add to a pan with sufficient water to cover them. Bring to boil, cover and simmer for 15–20 minutes. Drain and pound. Beat in margarine, seasoning and horehound. Cool slightly, and roll into balls. Coat with egged breadcrumbs, and chill.

In a deep pan fry parsnip balls in hot oil for 2–3 minutes until golden. Serve with the cooked beef and fresh bread rolls. I use this method with Jerusalem artichokes, scorzonera and seakale. For a main course dish, the rolls can be replaced by jacket potatoes.

With a green salad – part from the garden, part from the greenhouse – this dish can be served cold or hot.

Roly-Poly Sausage

Serves 8
1 lb puff pastry (prepared)
1 tsp thyme
1–1 ½ tsp comfrey, finely chopped
2–3 leaves feverfew, torn not chopped
1 lb beef sausage meat
3 oz Derby or Cheddar cheese, grated
milk to glaze

For the pastry, which I thaw the night before, see December. Roll out pastry to a convenient size. Mix thyme, comfrey, feverfew and meat, and spread on pastry leaving a 1 in. edge. Sprinkle with cheese, and roll loosely. Crimp edges firmly together. Brush roll with milk, and cut a line of ventilation slits in the top of the roll. Place on a baking tray, in centre of the oven, at 425°F (220°C), Gas Mark 7, and cook for 35–40 minutes.

If pressed I'd have to say my favourite vegetable is cabbage – green cabbage, not the red sort, which looks too much like beetroot. I'm told there are countries where the sun's too hot for cabbages. Thankfully, Derbyshire's climate means we can enjoy fresh ones all the year round.

Stuffed Cabbage

Serves 8
8 large cabbage leaves
2 cloves garlic, chopped
olive oil
8 oz brown rice
4 oz sultanas
2 oz peas
1 grated carrot
2 tsp paprika
1 tsp each of hyssop, tarragon and rosemary
sea salt
½ pint water
yoghurt and parsley to garnish

Blanch cabbage leaves in boiling water for 2–3 minutes. Drain and keep warm. Fry garlic in oil until brown. Add remainder of ingredients, and water. Bring to boil and simmer for 25–30 minutes, when the water should have been absorbed. Pour off any excess water remaining.

Place a generous spoonful of the stuffing on to each cabbage leaf, and roll up, skewering if necessary. Arrange rolls on a greased baking dish. Add a little water. Cover with foil and cook for 20–25 minutes at 350°F (180°C), Gas Mark 4. Serve hot with yoghurt and parsley garnish.

MAIN COURSE DISHES

Some November days never seem to get light. My mother called them the 'dull, dark days before Christmas'. Certainly the New Year never seems so dark. Each Sunday afternoon at Evensong first the nave and east windows darken, then the dormers. Oh, for those sunny summer evenings, when surely it never rained before dark!

A stew will cheer ourselves up with the thought that next month the days will start lengthening.

Short-Day Stew

Serves 4–6
3 lb stewing steak, diced
1 clove garlic, chopped
olive oil
4 oz carrots, diced
1 tsp stem ginger
4 oz sultanas
2 tbsp soft brown sugar
2 tbsp white wine vinegar
1 tsp rosemary
1 ½ pints beef stock
salt to taste

Fry meat and garlic in oil until brown. In a casserole dish add the meat and garlic to the other ingredients. Bring to boil, cover and cook at 325°F (170°C), Gas Mark 3, for 2 ¼ –2 ½ hours. Serve with jacket potatoes.

Perhaps it's the comfortable feeling of having sacks of waxy 'Red King' potatoes filling one pantry bench. When vegetarian friends are expected I sometimes make this simple dish, which they tell me they'll always come again for. When non-vegetarians come, I add salmon or chicken to the stuffing.

Stuffed Potatoes

Serves 6
6 large, smooth potatoes
For stuffing:
8 oz cream cheese
2 oz chopped nuts
2 oz sultanas
1 tsp parsley, thyme and tarragon, chopped
½ tsp coriander
sea salt

Wash, scrub, prick and bake the potatoes at 400°F (200°C), Gas Mark 6, for 1 hour. Cool slightly, halve lengthways. Scoop out the flesh and mash. In a bowl, mix the stuffing ingredients and blend with the mashed potato. Brown under the grill, stuff into jackets and heat well through before serving with swirls of soured cream.

When I was at school I hated the steak and kidney pudding, because it was far too heavily laced with thick, gristly-looking onion slices. But then, if you like onion, you may like to substitute it for my beloved garlic!

Steak and Kidney Warmer

For the pastry:
8 oz wholemeal flour
3 tsp baking powder
4 oz suet, shredded
1 tsp tarragon
cold water to mix

1 ½ lb stewing steak, diced
½ lb ox kidney, diced
2 tbsp seasoned flour
1 clove garlic, chopped
1 tsp rosemary
½ tsp each hyssop and thyme
1 oz sunflower margarine
salt to taste

Into a bowl sift flour and baking powder. Add finely chopped suet and mix well. Add tarragon. Mix with water to make a light dough. Knead lightly on a floured board. Pack into a polythene bag and set aside for 30 minutes.

Dice meat as finely as required. Seal with seasoned flour, chopped garlic and herb mix. Roll out ¾ of the pastry ½ in. thick, and line a greased 1 ½ pint pudding basin, allowing some overhang. Fill with the meat and herbs. Season, and add water to fill ¾ of the basin. Roll remaining pastry to make a lid. Crimp edges to seal. Wrap in foil and place in a large pan with 2–3 in. of water. Steam for 3–4 hours, adding water as necessary.

I like to serve this with French fried potatoes and a half-and-half mix of carrots and parsnips dotted with parsley butter.

DESSERTS

It was always a red-letter day when my mother baked her famous Washington Wish. The best thing about this Washington pudding was the way Mother was liberal with the ginger. I haven't her touch, but friends still come for it.

Washington Wish

Serves 6
4½ oz butter
6 oz demerara sugar
2 eggs
6 oz self-raising flour
a little cream
2 oz ground ginger
3 tbsp golden syrup

Lightly grease a 2 pint pudding basin. Cream butter and sugar. Beat in eggs and flour. Add cream to mix. Stir in ginger and syrup, and spoon mixture into basin. Tie up in a pudding cloth and steam in the top half of a steamer for 2–2¼ hours.

If, when serving, there's plenty of 'goo' at the bottom, it's a success! Serve with vanilla custard or ice cream.

I've said the only savoury dish I liked at school was Shepherd's Pie. Its sweet counterpart was Bread and Butter Pudding. It was really syrupy, with lots of sultanas. I don't make it often, since white bread's rare in this house. But family and friends love this pudding so, as a quid pro quo, I extract a toll of some plant or cutting for the garden. Shades of Llangollen! One day, I might try it with wholemeal bread. (see p.15).

Bread and Butter Pudding

Serves 6
8 slices white bread, buttered
3 large eggs
2 ½ oz caster sugar
3 tbsp golden syrup
3 oz sultanas
pinch of nutmeg

Cut the bread into strips 2 in. wide (or equivalent, depending on the shape of the loaf). Cover the bottom of a 2 pint oven pie dish, butter-side up, using half the bread.

Beat eggs into sugar, add half the syrup and sultanas. Spoon on to the bread in the dish. Cover with remainder of the bread. Spoon remainder of syrup and sultanas over the bread, and dust with nutmeg. Bake for 30–40 minutes, at 350°F (180°C), Gas Mark 4. Follow with biscuits and Stilton cheese.

When I'm on my own I have fruit as dessert for luncheon and dinner. Perhaps it's because we've always grown a lot of fruit – and, of course, in these health-conscious days it's certainly good for one. I love especially the red gooseberries, 'Whinham's Industry', which were here when we came. They're supposed to be sweet enough to be eaten raw, but even with my non-sweet tooth, that's not the case with ours. So, I make them into

Gooseberry Tart

Serves 6
7 oz wholemeal flour
salt to taste
5 oz butter
1 egg
1 ½ lb gooseberries
3 oz demerara sugar
cinnamon to dust

Sift flour and salt into a mixing bowl. Cut butter into knobs and rub in until crumbly. Add beaten egg. Roll pastry out on a floured board. Use ¾ to line a 7 in. pie dish.

Fill with sugared (*well*-sugared) gooseberries. Sprinkle with powdered cinnamon, and top with a lattice of the remaining pastry. Cook at 400°F (200°C), Gas Mark 6, for 20–25 minutes. It's wise to put a baking sheet on the bottom of the oven: on occasion, the gooseberry juices can overflow.

BREAD AND CAKES

Celery – the blanching and self-blanching – doesn't like our rigorous climate, but with the perversity common to gardeners we keep trying. At least more often than not we get a reasonable number of very slender stems – and they're the tenderest, anyway – just right for

Celery Loaf

I use the stalwart wholemeal bread recipe (see January), adding to each 1 lb of flour 3 stalks of celery and/or 1 tbsp celery seeds. It's a bread that's fine for salads, and to accompany cheese.

CAVEAT: Use only your own saved celery seeds, or those from health food shops, as the seed sold for growing in packets by seedsmen may have been pre-treated against damping-off and should not be used in cooking.

We don't have bonfires much less fireworks, which would frighten the animals, but we do love Parkin! 'Worth a guinea an ounce', my father used to say of black treacle – which was also Mother's sovereign remedy for coughs and colds. Perhaps that's why I rarely had either. I never make Parkin in small amounts. Try it, and you'll see why.

Hyssop Parkin

12 oz golden syrup
12 oz black treacle
1 lb strong plain flour
4 tsps baking powder
pinch of sea salt
1 tsp hyssop
6 tsps ground ginger
8 oz butter
8 oz demerara sugar
1 lb porridge oats
8 tbsp cream
2 drops vanilla essence

Stand the syrup and treacle in a basin on a warm surface to soften. Lightly butter a couple of 10 in. × 8 in. swiss roll tins, and line with greased paper. Into a mixing bowl sift flour, baking powder, salt, hyssop and ginger. Cut the butter into knobs and rub in until the mix is crumbly. Stir in sugar and oats. Pour in syrup and treacle. Blend in cream and essence.

Divide mixture between the tins and bake for 40–45 minutes at 350°F (180°C), Gas Mark 4. Score when half cool. Cut into slices when cold.

Probably because we're not a million miles from Scotland, St Andrew's Night (30 November) is celebrated in style round here. We have our own little supper party, which always concludes with glasses of apple juice and

Nutty Crunch

Makes 8
2 ½ oz butter
4 oz golden syrup
2 ½ oz demerara sugar
4 oz hazel nuts, chopped
2 oz walnuts, chopped
4 oz rolled oats

In a saucepan gently heat butter, syrup and sugar. Stir in the nuts and oats. Press the crunch into a 7 in. or 8 in. square non-stick sandwich tin. Cook at 350°F (180°C), Gas Mark 4, for 15–20 minutes until golden brown. Score, and slice into eight crunches when cold. It also makes a nice, if shapeless, hot dessert, with vanilla ice cream.

Oh, November, how you drag us into winter! But in three weeks' time we'll have started back (or forward) to spring. Christmas will come, and the snowdrops are growing, the jasmine's in flower, the primroses are out in the lea of the privet-hedge . . .

HERBS OF THE MONTH

Comfrey *Symphytum officinale*
Hardy perennial, to 3 ft

Dioscorides used a substance called *symphiton*, but it's not certain that this was our comfrey. In Roman times *Conferva* probably was, since its name derives from the verb meaning 'to knit together'. Crusaders are often credited with introducing comfrey to England, after its value in field medicine had earned it the name Saracen's Root. Later, it was popularly called 'Church Bells', from the pretty-hanging clusters of pink or blue flowers. The early American settlers made sure this healing herb was in their luggage on the voyage to New Jersey.

Very young leaves can be chopped or shredded into salads, or cooked as a green vegetable in their own right. Use a very little water in cooking. Comfrey is rich in constituents (Vitamins A, B12 and C, potassium, calcium and phosphorus) and contains as much protein in its leaf structure as soya beans (35 per cent). The young stems can be blanched (use a large flowerpot or cardboard 'chimney') and cooked like asparagus. Mixed with lemon balm and yarrow, it makes a refreshing tea; in winter, add a dash of honey.

Gerard says of comfrey: 'A salve concocted from the fresh herb will certainly tend to promote the healing of bruised and broken parts.' The common names of Knitbone and Boneset derive from the days when the pounded root mixed with a little water was applied to broken limbs, round which it set with the firmness of plaster of Paris. The mucilage in the comfrey, when mixed with water, formed a gel which was held to promote tissue healing. Today, the fresh leaves are used as a poultice for sprains and twists, delicate skins benefitting from an intermediate cloth to prevent the herb's leaf-hairs causing irritation.

A long-term remedy for skin ailments: pack shredded comfrey leaves into a dark jar. Seal for two years, then pour off the 'oil' into screwtop jars, and apply when needed. Use the sediment in the dark jar as a feed for houseplants.

A yellow dye is produced from the fresh flowers and leaves, using an alum mordant. In addition, comfrey is used in many animal feeds; formerly it was thought to ward off foot and mouth disease.

Comfrey is deep-rooting (to 10 ft or more), and is thus useful for bringing deep-seated nutrients to higher soil levels. Beg or buy divisions, as seedlings take several years to mature. Spring is the best time for harvesting the roots. Once established, you'll have comfrey for life.

For a high-potash mulch, wilt the leaves and strew them along the vegetable rows, or between plants in the flower borders: tomatoes in particular benefit from a comfrey feed. A liquid feed can be prepared by steeping some of the leaves in a butt or bucket of water, and using the resulting amber-coloured (and smelly!) liquid as a weekly summer feed for plants of all kinds.

CAVEAT: If taken regularly internally over a long period, a toxic alkaloid in comfrey may cause damage to the liver. Treat this valuable herb with respect.

Horehound *Marrubium vulgare*
Tender perennial, to 2 ½ ft

The Egyptians knew the value of treating coughs with despatch – and not much despatches a hacker like horehound. Not much tastes worse, either: the name 'marrubium' was emphasized by Pliny, who apparently liked his medicines less bitter.

This herb freezes well, so cut a bagful for the freezer before growth slows down for the winter. One leaf shredded over pork or beef, in the last 5 minutes of cooking, makes an ordinary dish special.

The leaves contain Vitamin C, and have been made into cough sweets, with a flavour all their own: an acquired taste. Chesty colds can be helped if you follow our grandparents' advice, and make a steaming hot mixture of horehound flowers and leaves in a basin. With a towel over your head, inhale the steam, 3 or 4 times a day.

The straightforward infusion, regularly drunk as a tea, does much to prevent coughs and colds in the first place. Friends to whom I recommended this, somewhat disparagingly call it 'Jungle Weed' – but have now been drinking it regularly for over a year, with beneficial results.

Horehound is an asset to flower-arrangers, not least for its attractive stems, which look as though they've been wrapped in cotton wool. As the summer advances, whorls of white flowers open in tiers along the stems, and attract bees. Take advantage of this, to help with the pollination of tomato flowers.

I grow this in a cold greenhouse, since its downy stems and wrinkled leaves are tolerant of low temperatures but not the prolonged damp conditions we suffer in the average winter. Given this protection, it's a cut-and-come-again herb, growing into a fairly large plant, taking up around 2 cu. ft of space after 3 or 4 years.

Feverfew *Chrysanthemum parthenium*
(Syn. *Tanacetum parthenium*)
Short-lived perennial, to 4 ft

This herb originates from Yugoslavia, its common name deriving from its propensity to reduce fevers. Three hundred years ago, feverfew was also used externally against skin blemishes, including freckles.

Its use in the kitchen is primarily as a grease-reducing agent, in fatty dishes such as sausage, duck or pork. But use sparingly.

If a few leaves are chewed daily (in a sandwich, if you find the flavour strong) over a period of months, it can reduce the misery caused by migraines. But, beware: in some cases it causes painful mouth-ulcers. One needs to decide then which is the lesser of the two evils. It's also one of the 'women's' herbs, an infusion of the leaves (vary the strength according to taste) promoting menstruation, and alleviating the tiresome one-sided headaches which sometimes accompany PMT.

The pungent scent of fresh or dried leaves repels insects – so rub it on the skin when gardening, or hang up in dried bunches indoors, to deter moths. Tuck some leaves under the mat in the porch, too, and enjoy the scent of the bruised leaves.

It's a herb that doubles as a worthwhile flowering plant in the garden. My own plants, in good soil and full sun (but no special feeding), grow to 5 ft and more, with many-branched sprays of tiny white daisy flowers which last for several months in the summer. There is also a golden-leaved form, which is a more compact grower. I site this near the front of the border, where it grows to around 1 ft in height and flowers only sparsely, its main attraction being in the foliage. In the wild feverfew is usually between 1 and 2 ft tall. It may be short-lived but it self-sows.

Hyssop *Hyssopus officinalis*
Rather tender perennial, to 2 ft

The name derives from the Hebrew *Ezob*, 'holy herb'. Hyssop was used in the ritual purifying of holy places, and for washing lepers, since a form of penicillium-mould grows on the foliage. In the first century AD Pliny mentions the wine *Hyssopites*, flavoured with hyssop. This is a recipe which the Benedictines inherited nine centuries later and converted into a series of liqueurs so delectable that very soon hyssop was a feature of virtually all monastery gardens.

The bitter flavour of hyssop is not to everyone's taste, so use it sparingly in the kitchen. The blue, pink, mauve or white flowers are pretty in salads. Traditionally hyssop has been used to bring out the flavour of apricots: add a wee sprig to flans and pies. Older leaves and stems can be used to rub on the skin of poultry, with a leaf or two added to meat pies and stews. Rich game and fatty meat can be digested better if a little hyssop is cooked with them.

A pinch or two of hyssop flowers makes a pleasant tea, which helps to relieve catarrh; but in general, today, hyssop is not much used in domestic medicine, having strong emetic and purgative properties as well as being an abortion agent. Containing ketones, acting adversely on the nervous system, hyssop should be avoided by anyone tending to epilepsy or nervous disorders.

Its essential oil is beneficial in aromatherapy, for the treatment of bruises.

In favoured areas, hyssop can be trimmed to form a pretty, evergreen hedge. North of a line from Bristol to the Wash play safe and over-winter this herb indoors, or take cuttings in early summer. A native of southern Europe, hyssop likes a light, fairly rich soil, in full sun. Bees and butterflies flock to it. Grow this herb near brassicas, to deter cabbage white butterflies; and around the roots of vines to improve the quality and quantity of the grapes.

December

'Emma' and Cats
King Sterndale -
December

And the shepherds returned, glorifying and
praising God for all the things that they had
heard and seen.
(Luke 2:20)

December

STARTERS

Cheesey Dip • Leek and Broccoli Soup • Fish Cocktail

SAVOURY LIGHT LUNCHEON/
SUPPER DISHES

Herb Pâté • Tarragon Eggs • Potato Gratin

DINNER (MAIN COURSE DISHES)

Turkey and Herbs • Royal Lamb Crown
• Rosemary Cod Steaks •

DESSERTS

Tangy Fruit Salad • Apple and Rum Custard
• Plummy Pudd •

BREAD AND CAKES

Sesame and Lavender Bread • Violet Sponge
Fruity Herb Cake • Puff Pastry

HERBS OF THE MONTH

Rosemary • Winter Purslane • Lavender • Bergamot

Except where otherwise stated, each recipe caters for four people

---

How I'd love to have heard the shepherd's conversation as they went back to their sheep, resumed their vigil, and waited for another dawn!

This time of year there are so many friends to send news, so many cards to choose and write . . . I work in three stages: Earliest to go are those to eastern Europe, out to the Asian borders, and to Australia. The next week sees the western Continent, Eire and Scandinavia. Then come the British – from Shetland to Ulster, and Cornwall to Edinburgh. Each day the mealtimes are dictated by the state of the 'in' and 'out' trays, and each day's shorter than the last.

STARTERS

Requests for articles on Christmas recipes come in, until I seem to spend more time writing about food than preparing or eating it. Early December's certainly good for the figure! With such a work-load this recipe isn't only a starter. However, since it's high in protein, who cares?

Cheesey Dip

Serves 8
4 oz winter radish, diced
2 oz landcress, chopped
2 oz hazel nuts, chopped
4 oz muesli
2 oz cabbage, shredded
4 tbsp winter purslane, chopped
2 tsp clear honey
1 lb soft curd cheese

Blend all the ingredients into the cheese, and serve in large scallop shells with toasted fingers of wholemeal bread.

If I was ever cast away on that desert island the luxury I'd choose would be a freezerful of Cheesey Dip. But the freezer would need to work on a battery, or perhaps by then there may be a solar-powered version . . .

Oh, I cheat here, and have several meals of this next recipe in the freezer! For this soup, choose the slender, most tender leeks – they've such an exquisite flavour.

Leek and Broccoli Soup

Serves 8
1 medium parsnip, diced
4 oz swedes, diced
2 oz butter
1 lb broccoli curds
1 lb leeks, sliced
2 pints chicken and garlic stock
3 sprigs rosemary
salt to taste
½ pint double cream

Wash and dice vegetables. In a deep pan melt butter and add broccoli and leeks. Heat gently for 3–4 minutes. Add stock, parsnip and swedes. Bring to boil and add finely chopped rosemary. Season, cover and allow to simmer for 20–25 minutes. Add cream just prior to serving with fried croûtons or fresh wholemeal rolls.

I didn't know her father, but it was a memorable day when I met Sir Frederick's daughter, Dame Kathleen Kenyon, at the Royal Society. We talked of archaeology in the Holy Land until well into the afternoon – long after my next starter and I had begun a tasty association . . . The recipe I make today is very similar to that first London one.

Fish Cocktail

2 oz lettuce or landcress, shredded
4 oz cod, cooked and flaked
4 oz plaice, cooked and flaked
½ a salsify root, cooked and diced
½ oz winter radish, grated
½ pint mayonnaise
parsley garnish

Using scallop shells, make a lettuce or cress bed. In a mixing bowl blend the fish, salsify and radish into the mayonnaise, and spoon on to the lettuce. Garnish with parsley sprigs.

LIGHT SAVOURY DISHES

Luncheon is the only meal this month with a chance of being taken in anything approaching daylight, but our dining-room is dark all the year round. So when less than six guests are lunching we use the south-facing library; scene of over 150 years of sermon preparation, and the writing of many theological treatises and theses.

It's a room where one of my professors, now the late F. F. Bruce, observing the perpetually-ordered chaos, once remarked: 'A misplaced book is a lost book.' Maybe – but, given time, it comes to light.

We manage to eat an unbelievable amount of this pâté over Christmas. I'm always modifying the recipe, but basically it's as follows.

Herb Pâté

2 garlic cloves, chopped
1 lb turkey, game, chicken or pigs' livers
5 oz butter
1 fl. oz cream
2 fl. oz sherry
1 ½ tbsp mixed herbs (e.g. thyme, parsley, balm and hyssop)
sea salt to taste

Fry garlic and liver in 1 oz butter. Melt remaining butter and blend all ingredients to required texture. Pack into ramekins and set aside in a cool place.

Pâtés are usually starters, but we've found this one's meaty enough to stand on its own – as are

Tarragon Eggs

Simply hard-boil eggs, shell and roll in tarragon butter. Eat either with fresh wholemeal toasted fingers, or arrange on a bed of brown rice and sultanas.

It's amazing how the once-abundant potato stocks are dwindling, even allowing for the two sacks sequestered in the car boot to give the rear wheels extra traction on icy roads. Still, December must have its

Potato Gratin

Serves 6
1½ lb potatoes, thinly sliced
2 oz sunflower margarine or butter
1 garlic clove, chopped
4 oz Lancashire cheese, grated
pinch of winter purslane
salt to taste
1 egg
½ pint cream

Wash and peel potatoes, and slice thinly. Lightly butter a shallow oven dish. Line it with layers of potato and chopped garlic. Between the layers spread seasoned cheese and purslane. Finish with cheese on top, flecked with knobs of butter.

Beat egg and cream, and pour over cheese and potatoes. Cover with foil and bake for 1–1½ hours at 350°F (180°C), Gas Mark 4.

MAIN COURSE DISHES

We had a Public Inquiry in 1985, over a proposed industrial extension which would have put our tiny village in jeopardy. A year of suspense later, when the Department of the Environment decided in our favour, I converted the stable-yard into a courtyard in celebration. Here fruit, flowers and vegetables grow adjacent to the kitchen, and we can sit out, sheltered from every wind that blows.

And, when the rain's pelting down, it's jolly nice to have fresh food handy. Choice little gems, like my treasured Snake Lilies (purple and white fritillaria) grow here, too. But mainly it's herbs – for even in December this next recipe tastes better if the herbs are freshly picked.

Turkey and Herbs

If you haven't a pan large enough to boil your turkey, roast it – but go easy on the fat. The more herbs you use, the more such fat as is around will be offset. Cook with the bird (whether boiling or roasting) a choice from rue (sparingly), parsley, sweet marjoram, basil, bay and fennel.

For the stuffing (which I cook separately in the oven to eat with my boiled bird), use less sage than normal and include bay, mugwort, bergamot, myrtle and thyme. Tarragon sets the pattern.

2 lb pork sausage meat
3 tbsp tarragon
½ oz coriander
1 garlic clove
4 oz wholemeal breadcrumbs
1 egg, beaten
sea salt

Mix well together meat, herbs and breadcrumbs. Add beaten egg and salt. Cook gently for one hour at 325°F (170°C), Gas Mark 3, and let the top brown gently under the grill for 2–3 minutes prior to serving.

Lichfield, with St Chad's Cathedral (its three spires have earned it the title 'Three Ladies of the Vale'), has long been one of our favourite days out. When our village church was built in 1847 we were part of the vast Lichfield Diocese. Then along came Southwell (1884) and Derby (1927). But still today, with so much hived off, Lichfield is one of the largest sees.

It has Dr Johnson's House, birthplace of the great man – and lovely old bookshops where time takes a rest. And it was with friends in Lichfield that I had my first Royal Lamb Crown – a treat of a dish which graces many a table here.

Royal Lamb Crown

Serves 6
2 best ends of lamb
2 ½ oz beef dripping
For the centre:
1 clove garlic, chopped
1 oz sunflower margarine or butter
¾ lb turkey pieces, cooked
½ lb button mushrooms
3 ½ oz wholemeal breadcrumbs
½ lb blackberries
1 oz demerara sugar
1 tbsp each parsley, chervil, thyme, tarragon and rosemary
salt to taste
¼ pint chicken stock
1 egg
For the garnish:
8 medium-sized Jerusalem artichokes, whole

Trim the lamb and form into a crown. Heat garlic in butter, and simmer for 2 minutes. Mix other ingredients in a bowl, adding butter and garlic. Bind with egg. Spoon into hollow lamb crown, placed on oven dish. Wrap in foil, and cook for 10 minutes at 375°F (190°C), Gas Mark 5. Reduce heat to 350°F (180°C), Gas Mark 4, and allow 30 minutes per pound.

Meanwhile, lightly roast artichokes whole. Just before serving, spike each cutlet bone with either a whole or a halved artichoke – much tastier than the traditional paper frill!

Rosemary, one of the ancient Herbs of Remembrance, should be remembered a lot at Christmas. Try these delicious

Rosemary Cod Steaks

Serves 6
6 cod steaks
salt to taste
water
6 lemon balm leaves, shredded
1 tsp chives, chopped
2 tsp rosemary
¼ lb flat mushrooms, sliced

I use a shallow, non-stick oven dish. Lay steaks along the centre of the dish, just covering with salted water. Add herbs and mushrooms to dish. Bring to boil, then cover with foil and simmer until the fish flakes under a fork (allowing 8–10 minutes per 1 lb). Serve with French fried potatoes and winter broccoli. Any juices not absorbed can be saved for the basis of a fish soup.

DESSERTS

From childhood, I've never been smitten with the charm of plum pudding or mince pies, so our Christmas desserts are not all that traditional. For instance, blackberries and custard or ice cream are 'the' dish on Christmas Day – and many more pounds of this favourite fruit are eaten until, and beyond, Twelfth Night.

I keep at least one bowl of fruit salad in reserve, and another in preparation. The following is one of a range of variations I meddle with. Be adventurous, and aim for as much colour and variety as possible.

Tangy Fruit Salad

Serves 6–8
½ lb apples, diced
½ lb pears, sliced
½ lb peaches, sliced
¼ lb sultanas
½ melon, diced
1 banana, sliced
8 fl. oz grape juice
½ tsp each bergamot, balm, hyssop, caraway, marigold flowers, rose petals
(remove white pith at base)
coriander (for the tang)

Just mix, and match, and enjoy. Keep any added water to a minimum; make the most of the fruit juices themselves. Add a dash of clear honey, if you like.

The Fruit Salad above is a driver's dessert. For those guests who don't have to drive I make

Apple and Rum Custard

Simply allow ¼ – ½ lb very finely sliced apple rings (cored but not peeled) per person, and add rum to taste in the custard. Especially good before a long afternoon walk!

This next recipe reminds me of Flower Festival time in August.

Plummy Pudd

Serves 6
1 ½ lb plums
3 oz butter
3 fl. oz water
6 oz demerara sugar
2 egg yolks
4 tbsp wholemeal breadcrumbs
½ pint double cream
1 tsp lemon balm leaves
pinch of nutmeg

Wash and stone the plums. In a pan melt butter with water. Add fruit and boil gently until soft, stirring occasionally. Pound to a pulp and stir in sugar. Remove from heat and stir in beaten egg yolks and breadcrumbs. When purée thickens, set aside to cool.

Whisk cream, add finely-chopped balm leaves, and blend into purée. Chill, and serve in sundae dishes. Sprinkle with nutmeg on serving.

BREAD AND CAKES

Resinous branches of conifer scent the house. Large panniers of sawn logs stand in the garage. Posts are later each day, and cards, wrapping-paper and parcels all make this one of the most exciting times of the year – so thrilling, the days which seemed so dark and short in November fly past in a whirl of celebration.

A friend in Australia writes of temperatures in the nineties – but we in snowy Derbyshire can't comprehend Christmas in such heat.

Here is another wonderful bread, to mark this season

Sesame and Lavender Bread

Using the basic wholemeal bread recipe (see January), add 1 tbsp sesame seeds and 1 tsp lavender flowers to each 1 lb wholemeal flour. Mix with a little sesame oil, reducing the water needed. Brush oven-ready loaves with more oil, and dust with sesame seeds. Finger-lickin' good!

For many years the fragrant purple or white flowers of sweet violets have been candied. But in mild areas (or under glass) it's a shame not to use the fresh blooms, since this herb flowers throughout the winter.

Violet Sponge

6 oz butter
6 oz demerara sugar
3 eggs, beaten
6 oz self-raising flour, sifted
½ cupful violet flowers
apple or plum jam
icing sugar to dust

Cream butter and sugar, and beat in the eggs. Fold in flour and violets, leaving a few flowers over for decoration. In two 7 in greased tins, cook at 375°F (190°C), Gas Mark 5, for 20 minutes.

Spread apple or plum jam between the cakes. Dust top with icing sugar and dot with violets.

My Fruity Herb Cake is eaten on New Year's Eve, with apple juice and gallons of thick black coffee-and-ice cream, Russian style. It ensures we all remember the night before!

Fruity Herb Cake

3 oz butter
8 oz self-raising flour
salt to taste
3 oz demerara sugar
4 oz sultanas
2 eggs, beaten
a little milk
1 tsp each of chervil, caraway and lemon verbena
1 tsp ground ginger

Rub fat into flour and salt. Add sugar and fruit. Beat in eggs and mix with a little milk if necessary. Stir in herbs and ginger. Spoon mixture into a greased 7 in. tin. Cook at 350°F (180°C), Gas Mark 4, for 1–1¼ hours. Serve with a brandy, or plain custard.

This is my favourite pastry, but it's so time-consuming to prepare I cheat abominably, making a lot at a time and storing several batches in the freezer. There may be those cooks who have half a day to prepare a meal. I envy them. Their daily schedule is so far beyond me!

Puff Pastry

I make my puff pastry in multiples of:
1 lb plain flour
2 tsp sea salt
1 lb butter
½ pint cold water
1 tsp orange juice (or lemon)

Depending on the dishes I have in mind for the pastry, I may add some chopped mint (which goes beautifully with the orange), thyme, parsley or lemon balm: just a pinch, that's all.

Into a large bowl sift flour and salt. Cut 4 oz butter into knobs and rub into flour. Add water and orange juice (and herbs, if used) and mix to an elastic dough. On a floured board, knead dough until smooth. Shape into a bun, and with a knife score a deep cross on it, to half its depth. Pull open the four 'flaps', and roll them out until the centre of the dough is four times as thick as the flaps.

Into the centre of the dough, shape the remaining 8 oz of butter. Fold the flaps inwards over the butter, crimping the edges gently with the fingers. Roll out dough to a rectangle roughly 16 in. × 9 in., using a light touch or the butter will ooze out. Fold the rectangle into 3 and crimp edges gently. Seal in a polythene bag and leave in a cool place for 20 minutes. Repeat this process 4 times, half-turning the dough through 90 degrees prior to each rolling.

If cooking the same day, chill the dough for 30 minutes before using. Otherwise, store in the freezer in polythene bags for future use. If you succeed in timing precisely each 20-minute slot, you must surely work in computers!

So now the year has come to its end. Thank you for coming through these months with me. We began as strangers, we end as friends – for we have eaten and drunk together. Perhaps we shall meet another day. Until then, let's pray with St Thomas Aquinas:

Bestow on me, O Lord my God,
an understanding that knows you,
wisdom in finding you,
a way of life that is pleasing to you,
perseverance that patiently waits for you,
and confidence that I may meet you
at the end.

HERBS OF THE MONTH

Rosemary *Rosmarinus officinalis*
Rather tender perennial, 1–5 ft

One of the many legends surrounding rosemary is that it never exceeds the height of Christ: after 33 years, it grows horizontally! The colour of its hazy-blue flowers is said to come from the Virgin's throwing her blue cloak over a white-flowering bush on the Flight to Egypt, whereupon the rosemary changed its hue. Rosemary was valued at birth, marriage and death: wrapped in a baby's christening gown, included in bridal wreaths, and strewn in coffins, placed on graves and carried by mourners.

Today, rosemary's pungency encourages wide, but cautious, use in the kitchen. A muslin bag of rosemary can be cooked with meat and vegetables, being extracted from the pan prior to serving. It takes away cabbage smells when cooking. Rosemary can be used fresh, dried or frozen. Try the leaves with soups (especially tomato), and a few flowers in salads, with cheese and in sponge cakes. Rosemary butter, with finely chopped leaves, is a tasty addition to jacket potatoes on a cold winter's day.

Its antiseptic properties made rosemary a favourite for burning in a sickroom, strewing on floors and in drawers, and being woven in the hair to ward off infection. Used in hair shampoos and conditioners, rosemary has long been valued as an antidote to greyness, and is a good scalp tonic.

Barbecue hint: if your feast coincides with a midge-infested evening, burn stems of rosemary, and the pests will fly elsewhere!

Take cuttings of non-flowering shoots in early summer, as an insurance against loss of the parent-plants in a hard winter. Seed can be sown in May, but be prepared for germination to be slow and erratic.

Winter Purslane *Montia perfoliata*
(Syn. *Claytonia perfoliata*)
Hardy annual, to 6 in.

Also known as Miner's Lettuce. The first generic name honours Prof. Guiseppe Monti, a botanist at Bologna in the eighteenth century. Many authorities, however, now list winter purslane under 'Claytonia', perpetuating the name of an American plant collector of the same period, John Clayton. This herb has for long been popular in the United States, but is now easily obtainable in Britain.

It's a valuable salad herb, being 'cut-and-come-again' in all but the hardest winters. All above-ground parts of the plant are edible. The leaves are tasty cooked as spinach, but their Vitamin C and iron content is best preserved when eaten raw. Allow the early, narrow leaves to be succeeded by the tastier, nearly oval second-stage foliage. Combined with early spring dandelion and nettle leaves, this makes a delicious and highly nutritious soup when there is often precious little else available in the garden.

An infusion of winter purslane can be useful as a blood tonic. Used cold as a lotion applied to skin blemishes, it promotes healing and toning of the tissue. Add fresh or dried leaves to the water for a refreshing bath, or a soothing bathe for tired feet. It used to be thought that an infusion of this herb acted as a pulmonary decongestant – hence the common name Miner's Lettuce. Certainly in the post-war years it proved a valuable natural source of iron, far preferable to the ubiquitous 'jelloids' of the early fifties.

Sow seed in late July or early August, as thinly as possible, since winter purslane doesn't like being transplanted and more quickly runs to seed if overcrowded. Once established, it will self-sow freely. Give this herb partial shade, and a rich, moist soil. Extend its season by sowing thinly in pots for a windowsill or greenhouse, if you live in an area where the ground is likely to be snowbound for any length of time.

Lavender *Lavandula officinalis*
Small bush, to 2 ft

L. officinalis is just one of the many lavenders available today. So if this is one of your favourite scents, why not shop around for varieties and start a lavender collection?

Lavender-water was added to the bathwater in Roman and Greek households (*lavare* in Latin means 'to wash'). We've come to think of it as typically English (and *L. vera*, the 'Olde English Lavender', has the strongest scent), but lavender is really a native of the Mediterranean countries – which probably accounts for it not being hardy in the colder winters in my garden at 1,200 ft above sea-level.

I love Lavender Custard (normal custard with 1–1 ½ tsps lavender flowers added). I also use the flowers in green and fruit salads, in jellies and blancmanges – and they give a piquancy to roast meat and game. Float a few in summer drinks, too.

In the garden, I can never get lavender to survive one of our Derbyshire winters, and envy more southern growers with their sumptuous hedges of this herb. But my bonus is that I always have a pot or two to hand, without having to brave snow or frost to pick winter leaves, which I use in tussie-mussies, as well as with meat dishes, all the year round.

Give lavender a light, sandy soil and full sun – but pot up a few cuttings as an insurance each autumn. When cutting the stems, take care not to cut too low, for lavender's one of those woody little bush-herbs that dies out if the clipping goes down into mature wood.

Lavender's antiseptic properties were perhaps first discovered in the Middle Ages, when – particularly on the Continent – it was carried to ward off plague and pestilence; a practice which today has the whiff of aromatherapy. It has more recently been used in a lotion for treating minor cuts. Lay the fresh flowering stems on the forehead, when suffering from a headache.

Izaak Walton, of *Compleat Angling* fame, had a penchant for lavender-scented sheets: presumably they helped him to sleep. Today, fields of lavender – for so long a part of the French scene – are being grown in southern England, mainly for the perfume and cosmetic industry. Homegrown lavender can be cut when the flowers are nearing their peak, dried, and used in *pot-pourris* and sachets.

Lavender seeds burnt in candles, give the room a lovely fragrance: soften the wax in gentle heat, and carefully press in the seeds. Allow to harden before use.

Bergamot *Monarda didyma*
Hardy perennial, to 3 ft

One of the herbs sent to Europe as seed by settlers in North America. The name honours Dr Nicholas de Monardes, a medical botanist of Seville, who included it in his herbal (*Joyful News out of the New Founde World*) on American plants of 1569. The common name derives from *Citrus bergamia*, a small Italian orange with similar leaves and scent. Bergamot's introduction to Britain came around 1745.

Oswego (Bergamot) Tea had been popular with the Oswego Indians; the name derives from the area by the Oswego River, near Lake Ontario, where the herb flourished. The beverage became even better known in New England after the Boston Tea fracas in 1773, when it largely replaced imported tea.

The flowers are attractive added to salads and fruit cups. The leaves can be cooked with fatty meat, particularly pork, and shredded into soups, stews, gravies and sauces; they also add spice to jams, fruit pies, jellies, savoury and fruit salads. To make the tea, use 3 tsp fresh or 1 tsp dried leaves, to a cup of boiling water.

The tea is good for coughs, colds and chest complaints, for bergamot contains an antiseptic related to thymol. It also relieves flatulence, nausea and menstrual pains. Inhale the steam to alleviate sore throats and bronchial catarrh. An ointment from bergamot used to be made to treat skin problems.

The flowers were formerly boiled by Ponca and Omaha Indians, for use as a hair-oil. Today the oil is used in the perfume trade.

Cut the pretty red flowers for long-lasting colour in arrangements, or dry them for *pot-pourris*, sachets, pillows and cushions. In the garden, they attract bumble-bees. Southern gardeners will also find they are favourite roosts of earwigs, so shake and wash carefully before using in the kitchen.

Give bergamot a warm position, in full sun and a nice, rich soil. Propagate from seed or root cuttings in spring, stem cuttings in late summer. Divide the plants every two or three years, or they become woody. This herb is an asset to the flower border. Several varieties are available, among the best being 'Cambridge Scarlet', 'Croftway Pink' and a purple form, 'Blue Stocking'.

Flower-Power in the Kitchen

I've already mentioned some flowers which can be eaten – notably borage, and violets; but many more are edible. Care should always be taken, however, to ensure that the flowers have not been sprayed by chemicals.

Choose from the following, to brighten up salads, garnish a variety of dishes, add to long summer drinks, or crystallize for cakes and sweet decoration:

alyssum	coleus	hollyhock	pineapple sage
anchusa	cornflower	honeysuckle	primrose
basil	cosmos	hop	purslane
bay	courgette	jasmine	rocket
begonia	cowslip	lavender	rose
bergamot	dahlia	lemon balm	rosemary
borage	day-lily	lemon verbena	sage
burnet	dill	lilac	sedum
carnation	elderflower	lime	sorrel
chamomile	fennel	lovage	stock
chervil	forget-me-not	mallow	tansy
chives	geranium	marigold	tarragon
chrysanthemum	gladiolus	marjoram	violet
cicely	hawthorn	mesembryanthemum	
clove pink	heartsease pansy	mint	
clover	hibiscus	nasturtium	

There are basically two methods of preserving flowers in sugar: one hot and one cold, often respectively called 'crystallizing' and 'frosting', though many tend to lump the two together under 'frosting'. For both methods use caster sugar, and keep air around the flowers as dry as possible.

THE 'HOT' WAY

Rose petals and violets are particularly suited to this method. Violet flowers are crystallized whole. In the case of roses, pick each petal separately, and remove the inedible white pith at the base.

In warm water dissolve 2 oz gum arabic, and allow to cool. Using tweezers, carefully dip each petal or flower into the solution, making sure that all surfaces are coated, and shaking off any excess liquid. Over a papered tray to catch the surplus, gently shake sugar over each flower, and set aside in a warm place on greaseproof sheets to dry – this may vary from 2–3 days to 2–3 weeks, depending on the types of flower petals, the time of year, and the heat/dryness of the room. Store in airtight tins.

THE 'COLD' WAY

Use flowers which are dry, fully opened but not wilting. Whisk the white of an egg, and with an artist's paintbrush (sable hair is best) coat all surfaces of the flower or petal. With a fine sugar-sifter, dust all coated surfaces, shaking off any excess on to a papered tray. Lay the sugared flowers on greaseproof sheets to dry (2–3 hours).

The flowers are best eaten at this stage, while their scent is fresh; but they can be stored in airtight plastic or glass jars, in a dark place, for several weeks.

When using flowers in salads, whatever dressing is used, toss the salad before adding the flowers, or their colours will suffer.

For a varied supply of colourful additions to summer drinks, pick the flowers carefully when they are at the peak of perfection, discarding the inedible parts (bases of petals, hairy calyxes, etc.). Freeze them individually in ice-cubes.

Where to Buy Herb Plants

Plants and Seeds

Arne Herbs,
Limeburn Nurseries,
Chew Magna,
BRISTOL, BS18 8QW

Cheshire Herbs,
Fourfields,
Forest Road,
Nr TARPORLEY,
Cheshire, CW6 9ES

Hill Farm Herbs,
Park Walk,
BRIGSTOCK,
Northants, NN14 3HH

Plants

Barwinnock Herbs,
BARRHILL,
Ayrshire, KA26 0RB

The Herb Harvest,
West Lodge,
STOBO,
Peebles, EH45 8NY

Seeds

Bethnei Herbs,
Thackeray Walk,
STAFFORD,
Staffs, ST17 9SE

Samuel Dobie & Son, Ltd.,
Broomhill Way,
TORQUAY,
Devon, TQ2 7QW

Mr Fothergill's Seeds,
Kentford,
NEWMARKET,
Suffolk, CB8 7QB

S. E. Marshall & Co., Ltd,
WISBECH,
Cambridgeshire, PE13 2RF

Suttons Seeds Ltd.,
Hele Road,
TORQUAY,
Devon, TQ2 7QJ

Thompson & Morgan
(Ipswich) Ltd.,
Poplar Lane,
IPSWICH,
Suffolk, IP8 3BU

Unwins Seeds, Ltd,
Mail Order Dept,
HISTON,
Cambridge, CB4 4ZZ

Indexes

RECIPES

HERBS